Dialogues Concerning Natural Religion

---

the posthumous essays
Of the Immortality of the Soul
and
Of Suicide

---

from *An Enquiry Concerning Human Understanding*
Of Miracles

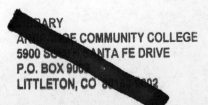

David Hume

Dialogues Concerning Natural Religion

the posthumous essays
Of the Immortality of the Soul
and
Of Suicide

from *An Enquiry Concerning Human Understanding*
Of Miracles

second edition

Edited, with an Introduction, by
Richard H. Popkin

Hackett Publishing Company
Indianapolis/Cambridge

David Hume: 1711–1776

First edition copyright © 1980 by
Hackett Publishing Company, Inc.

Second edition copyright © 1998 by
Hackett Publishing Company, Inc.

10 09 08 07 06   4 5 6 7 8 9

Printed in the United States of America

Cover design by Listenberger Design & Associates

Library of Congress Cataloging-in-Publication Data

Hume, David, 1711–1776.
[Essays, Selections]
Dialogues concerning natural religion and the posthumous essays,
Of the immortality of the soul and Of suicide,
and from An enquiry concerning human understanding, Of miracles
David Hume; edited with an introduction by Richard H. Popkin.
2nd ed.
p.   cm.
Includes bibliographical references.
ISBN 0-87220-403-0
ISBN 0-87220-402-2 (pbk.)
1. Natural theology—Early works to 1900.
2. Immortality—Early works to 1800.
3. Suicide—Early works to 1800.
I. Popkin, Richard Henry, 1923–
II. Title.
BL180.H78   1998
210—dc21   97-38335
CIP

ISBN-13: 978-0-87220-403-4 (cloth)
ISBN-13: 978-0-87220-402-7 (pbk.)

Contents

Introduction

David Hume (1711–1776) was an extremely influential philosopher of the Enlightenment, which was sometimes called the Age of Reason because many of its prominent writers applied reason to religious, political, social, and moral matters. Hume was notorious during his lifetime and thereafter for his criticisms of various claims to religious knowledge and for his naturalistic explanations of the origins of religious belief.

Raised as a Scottish Calvinist, Hume attended Edinburgh University for two years, when he was thirteen and fourteen. There he began to read the new philosophy of John Locke, and there he met some of the modern and moderate Calvinist thinkers. By the time he was twenty he had abandoned his traditional Calvinist religious beliefs and had developed the outlines of his general philosophical outlook. Shortly thereafter he used a part of his inheritance to go to France to write his first philosophical work, *A Treatise of Human Nature*, published in 1739-40. As Hume said, the work "fell *dead-born from the press.* . . ." By and large, the *Treatise* was ignored at the time; it has become recognized as a masterpiece only during the present century.

From Hume's letters we learn that the original first part of the *Treatise* was a critical examination of the evidence for religious miracles. So as not to incur the displeasure of Bishop Joseph Butler, a leading Anglican divine, he removed this section before the book was published. Hume said that he castrated the book of its nobler parts. Nonetheless, his skeptical attitude toward theological and religious knowledge gained him the animosity of the conservative Protestant clergy, especially in Scotland; his application for a teaching post at Edinburgh University was blocked by the opposition of these clergymen, who accused him of all sorts of heresies.

In 1748 Hume published *An Enquiry Concerning Human Understanding*. This in large measure is a more popular version of the first book of his unsuccessful *Treatise*. However, it includes both the essay "Of Miracles" that had been excluded earlier, and another essay, "Of a Particular Providence and of a Future State." These essays sought to show that insufficient evidence existed to support any belief in miracles or in providence and a future state, and that a reasonable person would reject all popular superstitions bearing on these matters. The two essays, especially the one on miracles, led to a huge number of attempted refutations; even in this century, some continue to be offered.

As Hume gained notoriety for his criticisms of religious views (he became known to the Scottish clergy as "the great infidel"), he also became extremely successful as a writer on matters social and political, and as the eminent author of a six-volume *History of England*, from the invasion of Julius Caesar up to the Glorious Revolution of 1688. His success led to a brief career in government: he served as England's chief representative in Paris, as the undersecretary of state for colonial affairs, and in various other posts. After leaving government service in 1767, he retired and settled down to the role of one of Scotland's chief intellectual and cultural leaders. When in 1775 he realized he was dying, he devoted his last year of life to completing the *Dialogues Concerning Natural Religion*, begun twenty-five years earlier. In this work, Hume tried to show that all arguments proving God's existence (especially the so-called argument from design) or establishing anything about his nature, were empty. His close friend, the economist Adam Smith, said in his account of Hume's last illness that Hume had stated that the only reason he had for wanting to remain alive was to see the elimination of the strange superstition, Christianity, that pervaded the world. Then, in his usual skeptical manner, Hume added that even if he could carry on his efforts in this direction, he doubted that Christianity would ever be eliminated.

The four works in the present volume are all central to Hume's campaign against organized religion. Only one was published during his lifetime. The three posthumous writings were composed or begun in the early 1750s, when Hume seems to have been at the peak of his effort to criticize religious beliefs. After finishing the two essays "Of Miracles" and "Of a Particular Providence and of a Future State," Hume began work on the *Dialogues*. Finding it difficult to produce rational arguments for the religious figures in this work, he asked a friend, the liberal Protestant Judge Gilbert Elliot, for help. Elliot's "help" was to tell Hume to stop, because his book would cause too much trouble. Hume followed the advice. However, two years later he prepared three more essays for publication: "The Natural History of Religion," "Of Suicide," and "Of the Immortality of the Soul." These were printed and a few copies distributed. Violent protests, especially in reaction to the essay on suicide, were launched by leading clergymen. Either Hume or his publisher decided that the better part of valor would be to withdraw the two most offensive essays, those on suicide and immortality. The *Natural History of Religion* was published without much outcry.

Hume then returned to further work on the *Dialogues*, which he finished in 1776; he made elaborate provision in his will to guarantee its publication. Although he did nothing to arrange for the republication of the two suppressed essays after his publisher refused to do the job, the essays were published a year after Hume's death. These three works quickly became known as major statements of his complete critique of religious views. The *Dialogues*, as the most extended and carefully presented picture of Hume's point of view, has been studied, criticized, and defended since it first appeared. Many consider it the most decisive modern critique of some of the major arguments concerning the existence and nature of God. Ironically, the two short essays, "Of Suicide" and "Of the Immortality of the Soul," eventually became the works of Hume most often reprinted. However, they have inspired relatively little discussion, either by Hume's defenders or his critics.

In the *Dialogues*, Hume realized several advantages in presenting his case through the dialogue form. First of all, in considering how touchy religious subjects were at the time, he was able by means of this form to avoid stating his own views openly; instead, he set forth questions and answers through the interactions of three principal characters: Philo, Cleanthes, and Demea. Each is used to point up weaknesses in the others' positions. As the dialogues proceed, it may appear to the reader that the skeptic Philo, who employs a great many arguments from Hume's other philosophical works, is slowly winning over Cleanthes and Demea, the two religious believers. However, at the end, Hume not only has Philo make what appears to be a confession of religious faith, but also has the minor character Pamphilus indicate that Cleanthes' opinions, which had been attacked at great length, are nearer to the truth than those of either Philo or Demea. This apparent contradiction leads to a problem in evaluating the essential message of the *Dialogues*. In what sense do they mirror Hume's views? One may ask, as several recent scholars have, who speaks for Hume, and what is being established in the course of the discussion. If we look at the last query first—what is being established through the discussion—we may come to an understanding of Hume's objectives.

In the Preface, Pamphilus tells us that the dialogue will be about natural religion, in contrast to revealed religion. The latter is any religion based on the belief that a deity has revealed himself and his will to mankind, whereas natural religion is religion based upon rational and scientific evidence and reasonings. It is taken as obvious and certain in natural religion that God exists; what will be explored is God's Nature and His Providential plans. (There have always been disputes about these matters.)

The dialogues proper, which are based in part on Cicero's dialogue *The Nature of the Gods*, begin with an argument over the unexciting question of whether students should be taught the principles of religion at the beginning or end of their formal education. The orthodox spokesman Demea and the skeptic Philo agree that religious principles should be taught last, after the student has been shown the uncertainties and contradictions inherent in all attempts to gain ultimate knowledge. Cleanthes then challenges this skeptical approach as well as the claim that religious faith can be built on skepticism. Cleanthes, representing such religious scientists as Sir Isaac Newton who found evidence for his beliefs in observations of the world around him,* also challenges whether anyone *can be* a genuine, complete skeptic, and whether skepticism can really support religion. After some debate, the participants come to grips with a central issue of the dialogues: Can we gain any knowledge of God's nature through science and sense observations? Cleanthes, opposing Philo and Demea, states *the argument from design*, which is supposed to establish both the being and nature of the Deity. This argument is based on inferring from what we see when we examine the world, which is a great machine subdivided into an infinite number of lesser machines. All these machines are adjusted to each other with overwhelming accuracy. Everything in nature is adapted to its function in terms of ends and means in exactly the same way that such an adaptation occurs in human endeavor, which involves design, thought, wisdom, and intelligence. Then, comparing the universe to human artifacts, "we are led to infer, by all the rules of analogy, that the causes also resemble; and that the Author of nature is somewhat similar to the mind of man; though possessed of much larger faculties, proportional to the grandeur of the work, which he has executed." Cleanthes insists that only by this argument—from experience—can we prove both that a Deity exists and that his nature has something in common with the human mind and human intelligence.

Cleanthes' argument has a long history. It was used in one form or another by ancient philosophers, and it became popular again in the seventeenth century, with the rise of modern science. Probably the most influential version of it appeared in the general scholium to Sir Isaac Newton's *Principia Mathematica* (1691). Because of

* "This most beautiful system of the sun, planets, and comets, could only proceed from the counsel and dominion of an intelligent and powerful Being."

Newton's status as the greatest genius of his age, the argument was accepted by a very large number of scientists and theologians, who kept looking for additional evidence that various aspects of experience were parts of machines like "human machines." They compared the world to a watch, and from that inferred the existence of a Universal Watchmaker. In Hume's day, one of the most popular versions of the argument was the massive compendium of evidences of design gathered by the Dutch scientist-theologian Bernard Nieuwentyt (1654–1718) in his *The Religious Philosophers: or the Right Use of Contemplating the Works of the Creator*. This was probably one of the works Hume used to develop his case. The book was first published in Dutch in 1714 and came out five times in English between 1718 and 1745.

The major part of the *Dialogues* is devoted to an analysis of the argument from design. Demea and Philo then indicate that the argument is both faulty and inconclusive. It is pointed out that from experience we know that human artifacts are the result of intelligent action; however, we have never had any experience with how universes are constructed. If it is claimed that we do, by analogy, know how universes are constructed, then Philo and Demea question the nature of such an analogy. The stronger the claim that human productions are like world productions, the more one is led by analogy to contend that the human artificer is like the world artificer. What does this lead to? The closer the resemblance of the human artificer to the world artificer, the more the Deity will be conceived to be like an ordinary human being, with all the faults and limitations of human beings. On the other hand, the weaker the analogy, the less we can know what the Deity is really like. Still further, it is brought out that according to the argument from design, the designer could be a fifth-rate deity, a superman, or even an animal or vegetable. The lack of information about the *cause* of the universe leaves us all at sea in trying to determine, based on our experience, what might be involved in the *construction* of the universe. From our experience, so many possibilities are conceivable that the argument from design cannot lead us to any definite information about a universal creator. Philo even raises the possibility that—if the universe can be thought of as having generated itself—there was not or is not a creator.

From all of this, the reader will probably accept the view developed in the *Dialogues* that the argument from design is neither logical nor informative. By applying the skeptical and empirical analyses developed in his other works, which showed that our knowledge was limited strictly to our experience, Hume points out through his characters in the *Dialogue* that we can gain no definite or even probable insight into the cause of the world from what we learn from our experience with causal relations in the world itself. Hume had contended in his major philosophical works, *A Treatise of Human Nature* and *An Enquiry Concerning Human Understanding*, that our causal knowledge is simply the recognition of constant conjunctions of items or events in our experience, coupled with the expectation that the future will resemble the past. However, since we have never observed the construction of a world or observed the world constructors, we have no way of knowing what causal relations might be involved in such a project; all we can do is construct hypotheses, without any way of judging which of these are more or less likely. Even the complete materialistic hypothesis—that the world is just the result of the fortuitous concourse of atoms—is a possible explanation, though Hume considered it a bad one. Presumably almost everyone of Hume's time would have been repelled by the materialistic hypothesis. Nonetheless, such a nasty theory is a possible one.

If the argument from design is shown not to be viable, is there any other way of gaining information by natural means about the nature of the Deity? Although Cleanthes and Philo briefly attack some other traditional arguments based on reason, Hume apparently did not consider these important. However, in the ninth dialogue he divided the orthodox viewpoint of Demea and the skeptical one of Philo, who had joined forces against Cleanthes' empirical theism. Now Demea argues for the traditional a priori proofs of a Deity. When Philo dismisses these proofs as poor arguments, Demea becomes incensed. When Philo suggests (in the eleventh dialogue) that God may not even be good, Demea finds "some pretense or other" to walk out.

Cleanthes and Philo, now alone, explore another way people have claimed to gain knowledge about the Deity—this time, knowledge of its moral character. An examination of the way that the elements of good and evil are distributed in the world may provide a clue as to whether the Designer of the world is benevolent, malevolent, or neutral. Once again Philo is given the more forceful arguments; he presses the case that we have no way of telling what moral qualities apply to the Deity. He insists that if we knew that God was all-good, we could account for the appearance of evil. However, we have to reason backward from our experience, which reflects a mixture of good and evil in the world. Philo contends that from what we experience, it is more likely that whatever being or force runs the world is morally neutral.

From this critique of what religious knowledge can be gained by human experience, Philo comes to a rather weak but positive conclusion. In the final dialogue Cleanthes had expected Philo to conclude in a skeptical way about claims to religious knowledge. Instead we find Philo saying, "That the works of nature bear a great analogy to the productions of art is evident: and according to all the rules of good reasoning, we ought to infer, if we argue at all concerning them, that their causes have a proportional analogy." What follows from this is "one simple, though somewhat ambiguous, at least undefined proposition. *That the cause or causes of order in the universe probably bear some remote analogy to human intelligence.*" If this appears out of character with what has gone before, at first sight Philo's almost-final words appear even more unusual: "To be a philosophical skeptic is, in a man of letters, the first and most essential step towards being a sound, believing Christian." The final words of the *Dialogues,* spoken by the observer Pamphilus, carry this mystery even further when he sums up the discussion by saying "that *Philo's* principles are more probable than *Demea's,* but that those of *Cleanthes* approach still nearer to the truth."

The thrust of the *Dialogues* seems to be to question and deny any claims to religious knowledge, especially those based on the argument from design. After this argument has been so deftly demolished, why should the skeptic Philo suddenly appear to accept a weak form of it that yields vague information about the Deity? Why should he next announce that skepticism leads to Christian belief? And why should Hume then have Cleanthes declared the winner? These apparent contradictions have raised the issue of who in the *Dialogues* speaks for Hume. We know that the problems involved here are most unlikely to have resulted from the author's confusion, since the *Dialogues* are the most carefully developed of all his writings; he worked over the material for twenty-five years, intensively so in his last year. His letters of that time show that he was fully in command of his faculties. So, we cannot explain these mysteries by attributing them to confusion, illness, or senility.

Part of the answer emerges if we look at what Hume said in his other critical writings on religion. In *The Natural History of Religion,* he declared on the first page that "The whole frame of nature bespeaks an intelligent author, and no rational enquirer can, after serious reflection, suspend his belief a moment with regard to the primary principles of genuine Theism and Religion."

Throughout the essay, written around the time that the *Dialogues* was begun, Hume contrasted the reasonable monotheistic view that intelligent people would accept—a view based on the argument from design—with the superstitious views of the general populace. Going further, Hume insisted even to the French Enlightenment atheist Baron d'Holbach that a reasonable person cannot be an atheist because the evidence of design in the world makes us believe in a *Designer*. Was Hume contradicting himself, simply ignoring his past writings criticizing the argument from design? I doubt it; and I think that there is a quite reasonable explanation.

In all his philosophical writings Hume insisted on the one hand that we are unable to supply adequate justification for our scientific, philosophical, and religious views, and on the other hand that we are nonetheless forced to believe all sorts of things. In the *Dialogues* this opinion is stated most strongly in the footnote in the middle of the twelfth dialogue (Hume added this footnote to the text shortly before his death): "No philosophical Dogmatist denies that there are difficulties both with regard to the senses and to all science, and that these difficulties are, in a regular, logical method, absolutely insolvable. No skeptic denies that we lie under an absolute necessity, notwithstanding these difficulties, of thinking, and believing, and reasoning, with regard to all kinds of subjects, and even of frequently assenting with confidence and security." Most dogmatists and skeptics might not accept this characterization, but it does seem to reflect the thought of David Hume, who spent his intellectual life showing that evidence to support or oppose knowledge claims was insufficient to justify or disprove those claims. However, Hume also recognized that he, like all reasonable persons, had to believe that the order found throughout the observable natural world indicates that the cause of this order should resemble somewhat the cause of order in the human world; that is, Hume acknowledges an intelligent being.

Hume's acknowledgment of an intelligent being may eliminate one set of apparent contradictions in his stated views. However, other contradictions remain, such as why accepting skepticism should be the first and most essential step toward becoming a sound, believing Christian. Hume certainly did not believe that anyone is forced naturally to believe in Christianity; the evidence indicates that he himself was an early drop-out from Christianity and that he never thereafter took it seriously as a belief that a reasonable man could adopt. His friend James Boswell tried to find some evidence that Hume had some Christian sentiments—and failed. Boswell, who visited Hume on his deathbed, found him as negative as ever about Christianity. What, then, accounts for the footnote added to the last dialogue? Actually, Philo was repeating what had been asserted by Christian skeptics from Montaigne and Pascal to Bayle and Hume. This view, which is close to that of Demea in the first dialogue, contends that because human intellectual resources are incapable of any certain truths, one therefore should abandon reason and accept truths on faith. This view, called "fideism," employs skepticism to undermine human knowledge claims in order to prepare the way for the acceptance of revealed truth. Various religious writers have stated this view in a moving and convincing fashion. In the course of the seventeenth and eighteenth centuries, some skeptics (including Bayle and Huet, both mentioned in the first dialogue) were accused of insincerity, of undermining both reason and revelation because, having cast doubt on reasonable knowledge claims, they also denied religious knowledge claims.

Hume sprinkled fideistic remarks throughout his writings. His opponents interpreted these remarks as insincere efforts to avoid criticism. My own suspicion is that they were intended to be ironic, to make the reader realize how silly religious belief was. Whatever the case, it is interesting that Hume's purported fideism had serious impact on some religious thinkers. One of these, the German philosopher J. G. Hamann, decided that Hume, intentionally or not, was the greatest voice of religious orthodoxy—for insisting that there was no rational basis for religious belief, and that there was no rational evidence for Christianity. When the *Dialogues* appeared, Hamann became quite excited; he translated the first and last dialogues into German so that Immanuel Kant might read them and become a serious Christian. Hamann's use of Hume as the voice of orthodoxy led the great Danish theologian Søren Kierkegaard to become the most important advocate of fideistic Christianity in the nineteenth century. So, although most of Hume's influence has been in creating doubts and leading thinkers to question accepted religious views, he also played an important role in the development of fideistic orthodoxy, culminating in Kierkegaard's views.

Moving on to the remaining question—in view of all that we have said—are we in a position to determine who speaks for Hume in the *Dialogues*, and to explain why the last remark in the text is that Cleanthes' opinions are nearer to the truth than those of the others? Scholars have debated the first question and are still debating it. It is not surprising that few if any claim Demea as Hume's spokesman.

Philo is the most logical candidate for this role, not only because he holds many of Hume's general philosophical views but because he seems to be the best debater (or at least is given the best ammunition to carry on the intellectual battle). Were it not for the last dialogue, most scholars probably would have chosen Philo as the hero. However, Cleanthes, who is not just a strawman throughout the earlier dialogues, does seem to represent an important point of view, that of the scientific believer. Hume, as a great admirer of Sir Isaac Newton, even said that Newton was the greatest genius ever produced in the British Isles. Hume saw that the religious view based on science (through the argument from design) had to be, or ought to be, accepted by reasonable men—as long as they realized how limited this view was. As Cleanthes moderated his claims and as Philo enlarged his, in a serious sense Cleanthes comes to represent a portion of what Hume really believed. In this case, Hume may be represented by different aspects of his characters, even by some bit of Demea's view.

Still remaining is the question of the meaning of the final line. Since this line is uttered by Pamphilus it may signify nothing of importance, for Pamphilus has no real role in the *Dialogues*. His assessment of win, place, and show may be interpreted as simply the appraisal of a stupid bystander—or it may be the assessment of a Cleanthesist. We are told at the beginning of the first dialogue that Cleanthes was the intimate friend of Pamphilus' father, and that Pamphilus is Cleanthes' pupil "and may indeed be regarded as your adopted son, . . ." With this close relationship, it is no surprise that Pamphilus thinks Cleanthes has the truer principles. But, one may ask, why does Hume give us such unexciting news as the conclusion of such an exciting work? It may have been for formal literary purposes, since the *Dialogues* begin and end with statements by Pamphilus.

Some have suggested that in the *Dialogues* Hume was trying to hide his real views and to forestall suppression, which did occur with the two essays, "Of Suicide" and "Of the Immortality of the Soul." I think that this theory loses its force when one considers, first, Hume's reputation as an unbeliever and as one who was even suspected of atheism; and second, that he left the closing lines untouched even after he had decided to publish the work posthumously. On the first score, even though Hume may have been a rather tepid deist who believed that some kind of intelligent force probably guided the universe, his opponents had labeled him an arch-enemy of established religion. It is doubtful that these people would be fooled into thinking that "the great infidel" was actually a true believer. Although Hume provided some crucial ammunition for Hamann and Kierkegaard in their defense of orthodoxy, neither his life nor his writings show any evidence that he espoused more than his very limited statement of the type of designer or designers that may direct the world.

The two suppressed essays, "Of Suicide" and "Of the Immortality of the Soul" show, even more strongly than the *Dialogues*, Hume's rational rejection of the central tenets of religious belief. After these essays were withdrawn from publication, Hume succeeded in retrieving almost all of the few copies distributed before the essays were to have been made generally available in 1755. Nonetheless, he worried about pirated editions coming out. On his deathbed he tried to persuade his publisher to bring out an edition, which the publisher refused to do. The two essays finally appeared in 1777, the year after Hume's death.

In just a few pages of "Of the Immortality of the Soul" Hume raises serious intellectual reasons for doubting that the human soul is immortal. In succession, he attacks the metaphysical, the moral, and the physical reasons that have been offered as evidences of our immortality. Basically, Hume's case against immortality is based on his empiricism. As he says near the conclusion of the essay, "By what arguments or analogies can we prove any state of existence, which no one ever saw, and which no way resembles any that was ever seen? Who will repose such trust in any pretended philosophy, as to admit upon its testimony the reality of so marvellous a scene?" Since Hume had shown that we have no basis for inferring the immortality of our souls from our finite and apparently mortal experience, he ends the essay with another version of his skeptical fideism: in view of the fact that we cannot gain knowledge of immortality by our senses or our reason, we must turn to Divine revelation for such knowledge. He does not add the implied conclusion: if there is any such knowledge to be gained.

The essay "Of Suicide" has been regarded as dealing with a more challenging issue. Both churches and civil societies have regarded and still do regard suicide as one of the worst crimes: suicides cannot be buried in holy ground; in most states a person can be arrested for attempted suicide or for conspiracy to commit suicide; and one of the very few reasons a person can be committed involuntarily to a hospital is if a doctor believes the person is likely to commit suicide. In the light of how the act of suicide was and is regarded,

Hume presented a most serious challenge to accepted religious and social views, in his argument that every person should be allowed to decide if he or she should continue living. Hume claimed that when philosophy is applied to a problem like this, philosophy becomes an antidote to superstition and false religion. The philosophical view of whether suicide is criminal depends on whether or not the act is a transgression against God, our neighbors, or ourselves. Hume argued that since human life depends on the general laws of matter and motion, it is no attack on Divine Providence to change the application of these laws. Since we can alter all sorts of natural events, states Hume, why not also those involved in sustaining ourselves? Why are we allowed and encouraged to alter the course of natural events for human benefit, and then told that changing our own nature by terminating a painful life is a rebellion against our creator?

When one considers the social effect of suicide, Hume argued, the man who retires from life does not do any harm to his society; he simply ceases doing any good. If a person can retire from any office in society, why can't he retire from society altogether? After arguing that suicide is not a crime, Hume concludes that "If it be no crime, both prudence and courage should engage us to rid ourselves at once of existence, when it becomes a burden. 'Tis the only way that we can then be useful to society, by setting an example, which, if imitated, would preserve to everyone his chance for happiness in life and would effectually free him from all danger or misery."

In a footnote at the end of the essay Hume directs his argument to the Christian view: he claims that nothing in Scripture prohibits suicide, and he contends that Biblical statements such as "Thou shalt not kill" apply to killing other persons, not to killing oneself. The pagans, Hume points out, saw that committing suicide was something heroic—why shouldn't we see the act in the same light?

Hume knew that he was dealing with an extremely touchy subject, and that he was challenging a basic assumption both of ecclesiastical and civil powers. In response to the very important issue that Hume opened up—whether a human being is entitled to take his or her own life—one Charles Moore, Rector of Cuxton, published in 1790 a huge, two-volume response, *A Full Inquiry into the Subject of Suicide*. He reviewed the discussions about suicide from ancient times up to Goethe's novel, *The Sorrows of Werther*, seeking to show that everyone who defended the right to suicide—especially David Hume—was monumentally wrong. The argument has continued in our own time. Almost all psychiatrists insist that anyone bent on suicide is mentally ill and should if possible be stopped, even if this requires incarceration. The chief medical opposition to this view has come from Dr. Thomas Szasz, whose criticism of the prevailing view is as sharp as Hume's, two hundred years ago. In a society which is gradually losing its traditional moral and religious restraints, the challenge of Hume and Szasz may become harder and harder to reject.

The essay "Of Miracles"

This essay is the first philosophical writing Hume did. It apparently was written shortly after Hume went to La Flèche, the Jesuit college Descartes had attended. Hume wrote his *Treatise of Human Nature* there. A Jesuit told Hume about a miracle that had occurred at La Flèche. Hume gently raised the point that no amount of testimony would suffice to make one believe that a violation of a law of nature had occurred, and that it would always be more likely that the testimony in favor of the occurrence of this La Flèche miracle was in error, than that the event had occurred. Hume said the Jesuit was shocked and said, "Sir, if you are right about this, then the same would hold for the miracles in the Bible."

Hume then went to his room and wrote out the essay. It was part of the original draft of the *Treatise*, but was removed as mentioned earlier before publication when Hume hoped that Bishop Joseph Butler would give a puff for his book. Only when he wrote a more popularized version of the *Treatise*, the *Enquiry Concerning Human Understanding* in 1748, did he include it.

The essay begins with the question of how we evaluate the veracity of human testimony. Hume insisted that we do it in terms of our experience of the course of nature. Very improbable testimonies can be accepted as we gather more information about nature and about the person giving the testimony.

In the case of miracles, reported violations of the laws of nature, can any amount of testimony make them believable? As violations of the laws of nature, the reported miracles would be contrary to all of our experience, since the laws of nature are generalizations of our constant regular experiences. Therefore it would always be more probable that the testimony about a reported miracle was false or doubtful than that the event had occurred. "[N]o human testimony can have such force as to prove a miracle, and make it a just foundation for any such system of religion."

Hume then used this analysis to attack those who think Christian belief is reasonable. In the closing section he contended that, in view of the miracles that a Christian has to believe in (and he just cited a list from the *Pentateuch*), which is more likely, that the testimony in Scripture is false, or that such miraculous events occurred. Hume insisted that any reasonable person would accept the first alternative. Thus, Christianity would have to be based on faith and can only really be believed on the basis of a miracle going on which subverts the believer's reasoning and "subverts all the principles of his understanding, and gives him a determination to believe what is most contrary to custom and experience."The argument undermining reasonable belief in miracles, Hume added, applies to claims of prophetic knowledge, since such knowledge is a form of miracle.

Hume's critique of miracles quickly became a central battle ground in the fight between religious believers and agnostics and atheists concerning the revealed religious tradition of Judeo-Christianity. From the mid eighteenth century down to today philosophers and theologians have been scrutinizing Hume's argument, and offering support or finding loopholes and ambiguities that might allow for some kind of religious knowledge based on miracles and prophecies.

In the *Dialogues* and the three essays, Hume exposed some of the raw nerves controlling the basic tenets of religious belief, and he made it clear that in several ways the bases of religious belief cannot rest on reason or experience. Since Hume's age, one of the strongest approaches of religious thinking has been to accept his claims and then to seek other bases for religious belief—to come to terms with Hume's criticisms without giving up the benefits of that belief. On the other hand, Hume has been a major inspiration to modern agnostics, who accept his criticisms at face value and who see no reason to adopt or retain any religious belief.

A Note on the Text

The present text of the *Dialogues* is that of Hume's own manuscript, in the library of the Royal Society of Edinburgh. I have modernized the text in four ways. First, I have used modern American spelling. Second, I have changed drastically Hume's use of capital letters to conform to common usage today. (Hume capitalized almost all nouns.) Third, I have modified the author's punctuation to make the text clearer to a modern reader. (The editions of the last forty-five years also incorporate such modifications. My text tries to preserve as much of Hume's style as possible while not making the work too choppy for today's readers.) Fourth, to ease the student's path in following the arguments throughout each dialogue, the speaker is identified in boldface type.

The texts of the two posthumous essays are taken from the original proof sheets, corrected by Hume's hand, in the collection of the National Library of Scotland. Again, capitalization and punctuation have been modernized.

The text of "Of Miracles" is reprinted from *An Enquiry Concerning Human Understanding*, posthumous edition of 1777. The spelling and punctuation have been modernized.

Throughout the book, unbracketed footnotes are the author's; the editor's footnotes are enclosed in brackets.

Bibliography

A. RELEVANT WORKS OF HUME

Hume, David. *Dialogues Concerning Natural Religion.* Edited by John V. Price. Oxford: Clarendon Press, 1977. (A critical edition with much scholarly material. The *Dialogues* was first published in 1779.)

Hume, David. *An Enquiry concerning Human Understanding.* Edited by L. A. Selby-Bigge. Oxford: Oxford University Press, 1966. Also edited by Eric Steinberg; Indianapolis: Hackett Publishing Co., 1977. (First published in 1748.)

Hume, David. *Essays moral, political and literary,* vols. 3 and 4 of *Philosophical Works.* Edited by T. H. Green and T. H. Grose. Aalen: Scientia Verlag, 1964. (These essays were published from 1750–1777.)

Hume, David. *A Letter from a Gentleman to his Friend in Edinburgh.* Edinburgh: Edinburgh University Press, 1967. Also included in Steinberg edition of the *Enquiry;* Indianapolis; Hackett Publishing Co., 1977. (First published in 1745.)

Hume, David. *The Letters of David Hume.* Edited by J. Y. T. Greig. 2 vols. Oxford: Oxford University Press, 1932.

Hume, David. *New Letters of David Hume.* Edited by R. Klibansky and E. C. Mossner. Oxford: Clarendon Press, 1954.

Hume, David. *A Treatise of Human Nature.* Available in edition of L. A. Selby-Bigge, revised by P. H. Nidditch. Oxford: Clarendon Press, 1978. (First published in 1739–40.)

B. BIBLIOGRAPHY ON HUME

Hall, Ronald. *Fifty Years of Hume Scholarship: a Bibliographical Guide.* Edinburgh: Edinburgh University Press, 1978.

T. E. Jessop. *A Bibliography of David Hume and of Scottish Philosophy.* New York: Russell and Russell, 1966.

C. WORKS ON HUME AND ON THE *DIALOGUES*

Battersby, Christine, "The *Dialogues* as Original Imitation: Cicero and the Nature of Hume's Skepticism", in David Fate Norton, Nicholas Capaldi and Wade L. Robison, *McGill Hume Studies*, pp. 239–252. Austin Hill Press, San Diego, 1979.

Chappell, V. C, ed., *Hume, A Collection of Critical Essays.* Garden City, New York: Anchor Books, 1966. (This collection contains, among other essays, three on Hume's religion, as well as R. H. Popkin's "David Hume: His Pyrrhonism and His Critique of Pyrrhonism," pp. 53–98.)

Gaskin, J. C. A., *Hume's Philosophy of Religion*, London, The Macmillan Press Ltd., 1978.

Hendel, Charles W. *Studies in the Philosophy of David Hume.* Indianapolis and New York: Bobbs-Merrill, 1963.

Hurlbutt, Robert H. *Hume, Newton and the Design Argument.* Lincoln: University of Nebraska Press, 1965.

Kemp Smith, Norman. "Introduction" to David Hume, *Dialogues concerning natural Religion.* Indianapolis: Bobbs-Merrill, 1977, pp. 1–123.

———. *The Philosophy of David Hume.* London: MacMillan Co., 1941.

Mossner, Ernest C. *The Life of David Hume.* Austin: University of Texas Press, 1954; 2nd ed. 1979.

———. "Hume and The Legacy of the *Dialogues*," in G. Morice, ed. *David Hume: Bicentenary Papers* (Edinburgh, 1977)

———. "The Religion of David Hume," *Journal of the History of*

Ideas, XXXIX (1978), pp. 653–663.

Norton, David Fate, ed. *Cambridge Companion to Hume*. Cambridge: Cambridge University Press, 1993.

Noxon, James. "Hume's Agnosticism." *Philosophical Review*, LXXIII (1964), pp. 248–261.

Penelhum, Terence. "Hume's Skepticism and the *Dialogues*." In David Norton, Nicholas Capaldi, and Wade Robison, eds., *McGill Hume Studies*. San Diego: Austin Hill Press, 1979.

———. *Hume: An Introduction to His Philosophical System*. West Lafayette: Purdue University Press, 1992.

Pike, Nelson. "Hume on the Argument from Design." In David Hume, *Dialogues concerning Natural Religion*. Edited and with a commentary by Nelson Pike. Indianapolis, New York: Bobbs-Merrill Co., 1970, pp. 125–238.

Popkin, Richard H. "Hume and Kierkegaard." *Journal of Religion*, XXXI (1951), pp. 274–81.

Stroud, Barry. *Hume*. London: Routledge & Kegan Paul, 1977.

Taylor, A. E., Laird, J. and Jessop, T. E. "Symposium: The Present-Day Relevance of Hume's *Dialogues Concerning Natural Religion*." *Aristotelian Society Supplement* 18 (1939), pp. 179–205.

Tweyman, Stanley, ed. *David Hume, Critical Assessments*. London: Routledge, 1994.

Wollheim, Richard, ed. *Hume on Religion (introduction)*. New York: World Publishing Co., 1963.

Yandell, Keith E. "Hume on Religious Belief." In D. W. Livingston and J. T. King, ed., *Hume: A Re-evaluation*. New York: Fordham University Press, 1976, pp. 109–125.

———. *Hume's "Implacable Mystery", His Views on Religion*. Philadelphia: Temple University Press, 1990.

D. RELEVANT TO HUME'S ESSAY, "OF SUICIDE."

Alvarez, Alfred. *The Savage God.* New York: Random House, 1972.

Plath, Sylvia. *The Bell Jar.* New York: Harper and Row, 1971.

Szasz, Thomas. "The Ethics of Suicide." In *The Theology of Medicine.* New York: Harper and Row, 1977, pp. 68–85.

E. RELEVANT TO HUME'S ESSAY, "OF MIRACLES."

Fogelin, Robert. "What Hume actually said about Miracles." *Hume Studies,* 16:1990, 81–86.

Lewis, C. S. *Miracles, A preliminary study,* chap. 13. New York: Macmillan, 1947. A major religious answer to Hume.

Merrill, Kenneth. "Hume's 'Of Miracles', Peirce and the Balancing of Likelihood." *Journal of the History of Philosophy,* 29:1991, 85–113.

Taylor, A. E. *David Hume and the Miraculous.* Cambridge, 1927.

Whately, Richard. *Historic Doubts Relative to Napoleon Bonaparte.* First published in 1819. Edited, with critical introduction, by Ralph S. Pomeroy. Berkeley: Scholar Press, 1985. An attempt to ridicule Hume's argument by arguing that the same standards Hume used to doubt miracles would lead one to doubt the existence of Napoleon.

Yandell, K. "Miracles, Epistemology and Hume's Barrier." *International Journal of the Philosophy of Religion.* 7:391–417.

DIALOGUES

CONCERNING

NATURAL RELIGION

PAMPHILUS TO HERMIPPUS

Pamphilus: It has been remarked, my *Hermippus*, that, though the ancient philosophers conveyed most of their instruction in the form of dialogue, this method of composition has been little practiced in later ages, and has seldom succeeded in the hands of those who have attempted it. Accurate and regular argument, indeed, such as is now expected of philosophical enquirers, naturally throws a man into the methodical and didactic manner; where he can immediately, without preparation, explain the point at which he aims; and thence proceed, without interruption, to deduce the proofs, on which it is established. To deliver a *System* in conversation scarcely appears natural; and while the dialogue-writer desires, by departing from the direct style of composition, to give a freer air to his performance, and avoid the appearance of *author* and *reader*, he is apt to run into a worse inconvenience, and convey the image of *pedagogue* and *pupil*. Or if he carries on the dispute in the natural spirit of good company, by throwing in a variety of topics, and preserving a proper balance among the speakers; he often loses so much time in preparations and transitions, that the reader will scarcely think himself compensated, by all the graces of dialogue, for the order, brevity, and precision, which are sacrificed to them.

There are some subjects, however, to which dialogue-writing is peculiarly adapted, and where it is still preferable to the direct and simple method of composition.

Any point of doctrine, which is so *obvious*, that it scarcely admits of dispute, but at the same time so *important*, that it cannot be too often inculcated, seems to require some such method of handling it; where the novelty of the manner may compensate the triteness of the subject, where the vivacity of conversation may enforce the precept, and where the variety of lights, presented by various personages and characters, may appear neither tedious nor redundant.

Any question of philosophy, on the other hand, which is so *obscure* and *uncertain* that human reason can reach no fixed determination with regard to it—if it should be treated at all—seems to lead us naturally into the style of dialogue and conversation. Reasonable men may be allowed to differ where no one can reasonably be positive: Opposite sentiments, even without any decision, afford an agreeable amusement; and if the subject be curious and interesting, the book carries us, in a manner, into company, and unites the two greatest and purest pleasures of human life: study and society.

Happily, these circumstances are all to be found in the subject of *NATURAL RELIGION*. What truth so obvious, so certain, as the *being* of a God, which the most ignorant ages have acknowledged, for which the most refined geniuses have ambitiously striven to produce new proofs and arguments? What truth so important as this, which is the ground of all our hopes, the surest foundation of morality, the firmest support of society, and the only principle which ought never to be a moment absent from our thoughts and meditations? But, in treating of this obvious and important truth, what obscure questions occur concerning the *nature* of that Divine Being; his attributes, his decrees, his plan of providence? These have been always subjected to the disputations of men: Concerning these, human reason has not reached any certain determination. But these are topics so interesting that we cannot restrain our restless inquiry with regard to them; though nothing but doubt, uncertainty, and contradiction have as yet been the result of our most accurate researches.

This I had lately occasion to observe, while I passed, as usual, part of the summer season with *Cleanthes*, and was present at those conversations of his with *Philo* and *Demea*, of which I gave you lately some imperfect account. Your curiosity, you then told me, was so excited that I must, of necessity, enter into a more exact detail of their reasonings, and display those various systems which they advanced with regard to so delicate a subject as that of natural religion. The remarkable contrast in their characters still further raised your expectations; while you opposed the accurate philosophical turn of *Cleanthes* to the careless skepticism of *Philo*, or compared either of their dispositions with the rigid inflexible orthodoxy of *Demea*. My youth rendered me a mere auditor of their disputes; and that curiosity, natural to the early season of life, has so deeply imprinted in my memory the whole chain and connection of their arguments, that, I hope, I shall not omit or confound any considerable part of them in the recital.

Part I

Pamphilus: After I joined the company, whom I found sitting in *Cleanthes'* library, *Demea* paid *Cleanthes* some compliments on the great care which he took of my education, and on his unwearied perseverance and constancy in all his friendships. **Demea:** The father of *Pamphilus,* said he, was your intimate friend; the son is your pupil, and may indeed be regarded as your adopted son, were we to judge by the pains which you bestow in conveying to him every useful branch of literature and science. You are no more wanting, I am persuaded, in prudence than in industry. I shall, therefore, communicate to you a maxim which I have observed with regard to my own children, that I may learn how far it agrees with your practice. The method I follow in their education is founded on the saying of an ancient, *"That students of philosophy ought first to learn logics, then ethics, next physics, last of all the nature of the gods."*[1] This science of natural theology, according to him, being the most profound and abstruse of any, required the maturest judgment in its students; and none but a mind enriched with all the other sciences can safely be entrusted with it.

Philo: Are you so late, says *Philo,* in teaching your children the principles of religion? Is there no danger of their neglecting or rejecting altogether those opinions of which they have heard so little during the whole course of their education? **Demea:** It is only as a science, replied *Demea,* subjected to human reasoning and disputation, that I postpone the study of natural theology. To season their minds with early piety is my chief care; and by continual precept and instruction and I hope too, by example, I imprint deeply on their tender minds an habitual reverence for all the principles of religion. While they pass through every other science, I still remark the uncertainty of each part; the eternal disputations of men; the obscurity of all philosophy; and the strange, ridiculous

---

1. Chrysippus according to Plutarch, *De Stoicorum repugnantis.*

conclusions which some of the greatest geniuses have derived from the principles of mere human reason. Having thus tamed their minds to a proper submission and self-diffidence, I have no longer any scruple of opening to them the greatest mysteries of religion, nor apprehend any danger from that assuming arrogance of philosophy, which may lead them to reject the most established doctrines and opinions.

Philo: Your precaution, says *Philo*, of seasoning your children's minds early with piety is certainly very reasonable, and no more than is requisite in this profane and irreligious age. But what I chiefly admire in your plan of education is your method of drawing advantage from the very principles of philosophy and learning which, by inspiring pride and self-sufficiency, have commonly, in all ages, been found so destructive to the principles of religion. The vulgar, indeed, we may remark, who are unacquainted with science and profound inquiry, observing the endless disputes of the learned, have commonly a thorough contempt for philosophy; and rivet themselves the faster, by that means, in the great points of theology which have been taught them. Those who enter a little into study and inquiry, finding many appearances of evidence in doctrines the newest and most extraordinary, think nothing too difficult for human reason; and, presumptuously breaking through all fences, profane the inmost sanctuaries of the temple. But *Cleanthes* will, I hope, agree with me that, after we have abandoned ignorance, the surest remedy, there is still one expedient left to prevent this profane liberty. Let *Demea's* principles be improved and cultivated: Let us become thoroughly sensible of the weakness, blindness, and narrow limits of human reason: Let us duly consider its uncertainty and endless contrarieties, even in subjects of common life and practice: Let the errors and deceits of our very senses be set before us; the insuperable difficulties which attend first principles in all systems; the contradictions which adhere to the very ideas of matter, cause and effect, extension, space, time, motion; and, in a word, quantity of all kinds, the object of the only science that can fairly pretend to any certainty or evidence. When these topics are displayed in their full light, as they are by some philosophers and almost all divines, who can retain such confidence in this frail faculty of reason as to pay any regard to its determinations in points so sublime, so abstruse, so remote from common life and experience? When the coherence of the parts of a stone, or even that composition of parts which renders it extended; when these familiar objects, I say, are so inexplicable, and contain circumstances so repugnant and contradictory; with what assurance can we decide concerning the origin of worlds or trace their history from eternity to eternity?

Pamphilus: While *Philo* pronounced these words, I could observe a smile in the countenance both of *Demea* and *Cleanthes*. That of *Demea* seemed to imply an unreserved satisfaction in the doctrines delivered; but in *Cleanthes'* features I could distinguish an air of finesse, as if he perceived some raillery or artificial malice in the reasonings of *Philo*.

Cleanthes: You propose then, *Philo*, said *Cleanthes*, to erect religious faith on philosophical skepticism; and you think that, if certainty or evidence be expelled from every other subject of inquiry, it will all retire to these theological doctrines, and there acquire a superior force and authority. Whether your skepticism be as absolute and sincere as you pretend, we shall learn by and by, when the company breaks up; we shall then see whether you go out at the door or the window, and whether you really doubt if your body has gravity or can be injured by its fall, according to popular opinion derived from our fallacious senses and more fallacious experience. And this consideration, *Demea*, may, I think, fairly serve to abate our ill-will to this humorous sect of the skeptics. If they be thoroughly in earnest, they will not long trouble the world with their doubts, cavils, and disputes; if they be only in jest, they are, perhaps, bad railers, but can never be very dangerous, either to the state, to philosophy, or to religion.

In reality, *Philo*, continued he, it seems certain that, though a man in a flush of humor, after intense reflection on the many contradictions and imperfections of human reason, may entirely renounce all belief and opinion, it is impossible for him to persevere in this total skepticism or make it appear in his conduct for a few hours. External objects press in upon him: Passions solicit him: His philosophical melancholy dissipates; and even the utmost violence upon his own temper will not be able, during any time, to preserve the poor appearance of skepticism. And for what reason impose on himself such a violence? This is a point in which it will be impossible for him ever to satisfy himself, consistently with his skeptical principles. So that, upon the whole, nothing could be more ridiculous than the principles of the ancient *Pyrrhonians*; if, in reality, they endeavored, as is pretended, to extend throughout the same skepticism which they had learned from the declamations of their school, and which they ought to have confined to them.

In this view, there appears a great resemblance between the sects of the *Stoics* and *Pyrrhonians*, though perpetual antagonists; and both of them seem founded on this erroneous maxim: that what a man can perform sometimes, and in some dispositions, he can perform always and in every disposition. When the mind, by *Stoical* reflections, is elevated into a sublime enthusiasm of virtue and strongly smit with any *species* of honor or public good, the utmost bodily pain and sufferings will not prevail over such a high sense of duty; and it is possible, perhaps, by its means, even to smile and exult in the midst of tortures. If this sometimes may be the case in fact and reality, much more may a philosopher, in his school or even in his closet, work himself up to such an enthusiasm, and support, in imagination, the acutest pain or most calamitous event which he can possibly conceive. But how shall he support this enthusiasm itself? The bent of his mind relaxes and cannot be recalled at pleasure; avocations lead him astray; misfortunes attack him unawares; and the *philosopher* sinks, by degrees, into the *plebeian*.

Philo: I allow of your comparison between the *Stoics* and *Skeptics*, replied *Philo*. But you may observe, at the same time, that though the mind cannot, in *Stoicism*, support the highest flights of philosophy, yet, even when it sinks lower, it still retains somewhat of its former disposition; and the effects of the *Stoic's* reasoning will appear in his conduct in common life, and through the whole tenor of his actions. The ancient schools, particularly that of *Zeno*, produced examples of virtue and constancy which seem astonishing to present times.

> Vain Wisdom all and false Philosophy.
> Yet with a pleasing sorcery could charm
> Pain, for a while, or anguish; and excite
> Fallacious Hope, or arm the obdurate breast
> With stubborn Patience, as with triple steel.[2]

In like manner, if a man has accustomed himself to skeptical considerations on the uncertainty and narrow limits of reason, he will not entirely forget them when he turns his reflection on other subjects; but in all his philosophical principles and reasoning, I dare not say, in his common conduct, he will be found different from those who either never formed any opinions in the case or have entertained sentiments more favorable to human reason.

To whatever length anyone may push his speculative principles of skepticism, he must act, I own, and live, and converse like other men; and for this conduct he is not obliged to give any other reason

2. [Milton, *Paradise Lost*, Bk. II.]

than the absolute necessity he lies under of so doing. If he ever carries his speculations farther than this necessity constrains him, and philosophizes either on natural or moral subjects, he is allured by a certain pleasure and satisfaction which he finds in employing himself after that manner. He considers, besides, that everyone, even in common life, is constrained to have more or less of this philosophy; that from our earliest infancy we make continual advances in forming more general principles of conduct and reasoning; that the larger experience we acquire, and the stronger reason we are endued with, we always render our principles the more general and comprehensive; and that what we call *philosophy* is nothing but a more regular and methodical operation of the same kind. To philosophize on such subjects is nothing essentially different from reasoning on common life, and we may only expect greater stability, if not greater truth, from our philosophy on account of its exacter and more scrupulous method of proceeding.

But when we look beyond human affairs and the properties of the surrounding bodies; when we carry our speculations into the two eternities, before and after the present state of things; into the creation and formation of the universe; the existence and properties of spirits; the powers and operations of one universal Spirit existing without beginning and without end, omnipotent, omniscient, immutable, infinite, and incomprehensible. We must be far removed from the smallest tendency to skepticism not to be apprehensive that we have here got quite beyond the reach of our faculties. So long as we confine our speculations to trade, or morals, or politics, or criticism, we make appeals, every moment, to common sense and experience, which strengthen our philosophical conclusions and remove (at least in part) the suspicion, which we so justly entertain with regard to every reasoning, that is very subtile and refined. But in theological reasonings, we have not this advantage; while at the same time we are employed upon objects which, we must be sensible, are too large for our grasp, and of all others, require most to be familiarized to our apprehension. We are like foreigners in a strange country to whom everything must seem suspicious, and who are in danger every moment of transgressing against the laws and customs of the people with whom they live and converse. We know not how far we ought to trust our vulgar methods of reasoning in such a subject, since, even in common life, and in that province which is peculiarly appropriated to them, we cannot account for them and are entirely guided by a kind of instinct or necessity in employing them.

All skeptics pretend that, if reason be considered in an abstract view, it furnishes invincible arguments against itself, and that we could never retain any conviction or assurance, on any subject, were not the skeptical reasonings so refined and subtile that they are not able to counterpoise the more solid and more natural arguments derived from the senses and experience. But it is evident, whenever our arguments lose this advantage and run wide of common life, that the most refined skepticism comes to be upon a footing with them, and is able to oppose and counterbalance them. The one has no more weight than the other. The mind must remain in suspense between them; and it is that very suspense or balance which is the triumph of skepticism.

Cleanthes: But I observe, says *Cleanthes*, with regard to you, *Philo*, and all speculative skeptics that your doctrine and practice are as much at variance in the most abstruse points of theory as in the conduct of common life. Wherever evidence discovers itself, you adhere to it, notwithstanding your pretended skepticism; and I can observe, too, some of your sect to be as decisive as those who make greater professions of certainty and assurance. In reality, would not a man be ridiculous who pretended to reject *Newton's* explication of the wonderful phenomenon of the rainbow because that explication gives a minute anatomy of the rays of light—a subject, forsooth, too refined for human comprehension? And what would you say to one who, having nothing particular to object to the arguments of *Copernicus* and *Galileo* for the motion of the earth, should withhold his assent on that general principle that these subjects were too magnificent and remote to be explained by the narrow and fallacious reason of mankind?

There is indeed a kind of brutish and ignorant skepticism, as you well observed, which gives the vulgar a general prejudice against what they do not easily understand, and makes them reject every principle which requires elaborate reasoning to prove and establish it. This species of skepticism is fatal to knowledge, not to religion; since we find that those who make greatest profession of it give often their assent, not only to the great truths of theism and natural theology, but even to the most absurd tenets which a traditional superstition has recommended to them. They firmly believe in witches, though they will not believe nor attend to the most simple proposition of *Euclid*.[3] But the refined and philosophical skeptics

---

3. [Hume is apparently referring to Joseph Glanvill, 1636–1680, a leading English skeptic who also believed in witchcraft and published evidence about it.]

fall into an inconsistence of an opposite nature. They push their researches into the most abstruse corners of science, and their assent attends them in every step, proportioned to the evidence which they meet with. They are even obliged to acknowledge that the most abstruse and remote objects are those which are best explained by philosophy. Light is in reality anatomized. The true system of the heavenly bodies is discovered and ascertained. But the nourishment of bodies by food is still an inexplicable mystery. The cohesion of the parts of matter is still incomprehensible. These skeptics, therefore, are obliged, in every question, to consider each particular evidence apart, and proportion their assent to the precise degree of evidence which occurs. This is their practice in all natural, mathematical, moral, and political science. And why not the same, I ask, in the theological and religious? Why must conclusions of this nature be alone rejected on the general presumption of the insufficiency of human reason, without any particular discussion of the evidence? Is not such an unequal conduct a plain proof of prejudice and passion?

Our senses, you say, are fallacious; our understanding erroneous; our ideas, even of the most familiar objects; extension, duration, motion—full of absurdities and contradictions. You defy me to solve the difficulties or reconcile the repugnancies which you discover in them. I have not capacity for so great an undertaking: I have not leisure for it: I perceive it to be superfluous. Your own conduct, in every circumstance, refutes your principles, and shows the firmest reliance on all the received maxims of science, morals, prudence, and behavior.

I shall never assent to so harsh an opinion as that of a celebrated writer,[4] who says that the *Skeptics* are not a sect of philosophers: they are only a sect of liars. I may, however, affirm (I hope without offence) that they are a sect of jesters or railliers. But for my part, whenever I find myself disposed to mirth and amusement, I shall certainly choose my entertainment of a less perplexing and abstruse nature. A comedy, a novel, or, at most, a history seems a more natural recreation than such metaphysical subtilties and abstractions.

In vain would the skeptic make a distinction between science and common life, or between one science and another. The arguments employed in all, if just, are of a similar nature and contain the same

---

4. L'art de penser. [*Port Royal Logic*, written in 1662 by Antoine Arnauld and Pierre Nicole, two leading Jansenist theologians. This work is strongly Cartesian. It was used as a textbook well into the nineteenth century.]

force and evidence. Or if there be any difference among them, the advantage lies entirely on the side of theology and natural religion. Many principles of mechanics are founded on very abstruse reasoning; yet no man who has any pretensions to science, even no speculative skeptic, pretends to entertain the least doubt with regard to them. The *Copernican* system contains the most surprising paradox, and the most contrary to our natural conceptions, to appearances, and to our very senses. Yet even monks and inquistors are now constrained to withdraw their opposition to it. And shall *Philo*, a man of so liberal a genius and extensive knowledge, entertain any general undistinguished scruples with regard to the religious hypothesis, which is founded on the simplest and most obvious arguments and, unless it meets with artificial obstacles, has such easy access and admission into the mind of man?

And here we may observe, continued he, turning himself towards *Demea*, a pretty curious circumstance in the history of the sciences. After the union of philosophy with the popular religion, upon the first establishment of *Christianity*, nothing was more usual, among all religious teachers, than declamations against reason, against the senses, against every principle derived merely from human research and inquiry. All topics of the ancient *Academics*[5] were adopted by the Fathers, and thence propagated for several ages in every school and pulpit throughout *Christendom*. The Reformers embraced the same principles of reasoning or rather declamation; and all panegyrics on the excellence of faith were sure to be interlarded with some severe strokes of satire against natural reason. A celebrated prelate, too,[6] of the Romish communion, a man of the most extensive learning, who wrote a demonstration of Christianity, has also composed a treatise which contains all the cavils of the boldest and most determined *Pyrrhonism*. *Locke* seems to have been the first *Christian* who ventured openly to assert that *faith* was nothing but a species of *reason*; that religion was only a branch of philosophy; and that a chain of arguments, similar to that which established any truth in morals, politics, or physics, was always

5. [The Academics were the dogmatic skeptical school that insisted that nothing can be known, in contrast to the Pyrrhonians who doubt even that.]

6. Mons. Huet. [Pierre–Daniel Huet, 1630–1721, was the Bishop of Avranches. He wrote a long apologetic work for Christianity entitled *Demonstratio Evangelica*, 1679. He also wrote a *Traité philosophique de la foiblesse de l'esprit humain*, 1723, an extremely skeptical work that appeared in English in 1725. Hume seems to have read it fairly early in his career.]

employed in discovering all the principles of theology, natural and revealed. The ill use which *Bayle*[7] and other libertines made of the philosophical skepticism of the Fathers and first Reformers still further propagated the judicious sentiment of *Mr. Locke.* And it is now in a manner avowed, by all pretenders to reasoning and philosophy, that atheist and skeptic are almost synonymous. And as it is certain that no man is in earnest when he professes the latter principle, I would fain hope that there are as few who seriously maintain the former.

Philo: Don't you remember, said *Philo,* the excellent saying of *Lord Bacon* on this head? **Cleanthes:** That a little philosophy, replied *Cleanthes,* makes a man an atheist; a great deal converts him to religion. **Philo:** That is a very judicious remark, too, said *Philo.* But what I have in my eye is another passage, where, having mentioned *David's* fool, who said in his heart there is no God, this great philosopher observes that the atheists nowadays have a double share of folly. For they are not contented to say in their hearts there is no God, but they also utter that impiety with their lips, and are thereby guilty of multiplied indiscretion and imprudence. Such people, though they were ever so much in earnest, cannot, methinks, be very formidable.

But though you should rank me in this class of fools, I cannot forbear communicating a remark that occurs to me from the history of the religious and irreligious skepticism with which you have entertained us. It appears to me that there are strong symptoms of priestcraft in the whole progress of this affair. During ignorant ages, such as those which followed the dissolution of the ancient schools, the priests perceived that atheism, deism, or heresy of any kind, could only proceed from the presumptuous questioning of received opinions, and from a belief that human reason was equal to everything. Education had then a mighty influence over the minds of men, and was almost equal in force to those suggestions of the senses and common understanding by which the most determined skeptic must allow himself to be governed. But at present, when the influence of education is much diminished and men, from a more open commerce of the world, have learned to compare the popular principles of different nations and ages, our sagacious divines have changed their whole system of philosophy and talk the language of *Stoics, Platonists,* and *Peripatetics,* not that of *Pyrrho-*

---

7. [Pierre Bayle, 1647–1706, was the leading skeptic of his time. Hume was much influenced by his writings.]

nians and *Academics.* If we distrust human reason we have now no other principle to lead us into religion. Thus skeptics in one age, dogmatists in another—whichever system best suits the purpose of these reverend gentlemen in giving them an ascendant over mankind, they are sure to make it their favorite principle and established tenet.

Cleanthes: It is very natural, said *Cleanthes*, for men to embrace those principles by which they find they can best defend their doctrines, nor need we have any recourse to priestcraft to account for so reasonable an expedient. And surely, nothing can afford a stronger presumption that any set of principles are true and ought to be embraced than to observe that they tend to the confirmation of true religion, and serve to confound the cavils of atheists, libertines, and free-thinkers of all denominations.

Part II

Demea: I must own, *Cleanthes,* said *Demea,* that nothing can more surprise me than the light in which you have all along put this argument. By the whole tenor of your discourse, one would imagine that you were maintaining the being of a God against the cavils of atheists and infidels, and were necessitated to become a champion for that fundamental principle of all religion. But this, I hope, is not by any means a question among us. No man; no man, at least of common sense, I am persuaded, ever entertained a serious doubt with regard to a truth so certain and self-evident. The question is not concerning the *being* but the *nature* of God. This I affirm, from the infirmities of human understanding, to be altogether incomprehensible and unknown to us. The essence of that supreme mind, his attributes, the manner of his existence, the very nature of his duration; these and every particular which regards so divine a being are mysterious to men. Finite, weak, and blind creatures, we ought to humble ourselves in his august presence, and, conscious of our frailties, adore in silence his infinite perfections which eye hath not seen, ear hath not heard, neither hath it entered into the heart of man to conceive. They are covered in a deep cloud from human curiosity; it is profaneness to attempt penetrating through these sacred obscurities; and, next to the impiety of denying his existence, is the temerity of prying into his nature and essence, decrees and attributes.

But lest you should think that my *piety* has here got the better of my *philosophy,* I shall support my opinion, if it needs any support, by a very great authority. I might cite all the divines, almost from the foundation of *Christianity,* who have ever treated of this or any other theological subject; but I shall confine myself, at present, to one equally celebrated for piety and philosophy. It is *Father Malebranche* who, I remember, thus expresses himself.[8] "One ought

8. *Recherche de la Vérité,* liv. 3, cap. 9. [Nicolas Malebranche, 1638–1715, a ma-

not so much (says he) to call God a spirit in order to express positively what he is, as in order to signify that he is not matter. He is a Being infinitely perfect—of this we cannot doubt. But in the same manner as we ought not to imagine, even supposing him corporeal, that he is clothed with a human body, as the *Anthropomorphites* asserted, under color that that figure was the most perfect of any, so neither ought we to imagine that the spirit of God has human ideas or bears any resemblance to our spirit, under color that we know nothing more perfect than a human mind. We ought rather to believe that as he comprehends the perfections of matter without being material . . . he comprehends also the perfections of created spirits without being spirit, in the manner we conceive spirit: That his true name is *He that is*, or, in other words, Being without restriction, All Being, the Being infinite and universal"

Philo: After so great an authority, *Demea*, replied *Philo*, as that which you have produced, and a thousand more which you might produce, it would appear ridiculous in me to add my sentiment or express my approbation of your doctrine. But surely, where reasonable men treat these subjects, the question can never be concerning the *being* but only the *nature* of the Deity. The former truth, as you well observe, is unquestionable and self-evident. Nothing exists without a cause; and the original cause of this universe (whatever it be) we call *God*, and piously ascribe to him every species of perfection. Whoever scruples this fundamental truth deserves every punishment which can be inflicted among philosophers, to wit, the greatest ridicule, contempt, and disapprobation. But as all perfection is entirely relative, we ought never to imagine that we comprehend the attributes of this divine Being, or to suppose that his perfections have any analogy or likeness to the perfections of a human creature. Wisdom, thought, design, knowledge—these we justly ascribe to him because these words are honorable among men, and we have no other language or other conceptions by which we can express our adoration of him. But let us beware lest we think that our ideas anywise correspond to his perfections, or that his attributes have any resemblance to these qualities among men. He is infinitely superior to our limited view and comprehension; and is more the object of worship in the temple than of disputation in the schools.

---

jor metaphysican, greatly influenced by Descartes. His most important work, *Recherche de la Verité*, appeared in 1674-75. Hume was greatly influenced by Father Malebranche.]

In reality, *Cleanthes,* continued he, there is no need of having recourse to that affected skepticism, so displeasing to you, in order to come at this determination. Our ideas reach no farther than our experience: We have no experience of divine attributes and operations. I need not conclude my syllogism: You can draw the inference yourself. And it is a pleasure to me (and I hope to you, too) that just reasoning and sound piety here concur in the same conclusion, and both of them establish the adorably mysterious and incomprehensible nature of the Supreme Being.

Cleanthes: Not to lose any time in circumlocutions, said *Cleanthes,* addressing himself to *Demea,* much less in replying to the pious declamations of *Philo,* I shall briefly explain how I conceive this matter. Look round the world: Contemplate the whole and every part of it: You will find it to be nothing but one great machine, subdivided into an infinite number of lesser machines, which again admit of subdivisions to a degree beyond what human senses and faculties can trace and explain. All these various machines, and even their most minute parts, are adjusted to each other with an accuracy which ravishes into admiration all men who have ever contemplated them. The curious adapting of means to ends, throughout all nature, resembles exactly, though it much exceeds, the productions of human contrivance; of human design, thought, wisdom, and intelligence. Since therefore the effects resemble each other, we are led to infer, by all the rules of analogy, that the causes also resemble, and that the Author of Nature is somewhat similar to the mind of man, though possessed of much larger faculties, proportioned to the grandeur of the work which he has executed. By this argument *a posteriori,* and by this argument alone, do we prove at once the existence of a Deity and his similarity to human mind and intelligence.

Demea: I shall be so free, *Cleanthes,* said *Demea,* as to tell you that from the beginning I could not approve of your conclusion concerning the similarity of the Deity to men; still less can I approve of the mediums by which you endeavor to establish it. What! No demonstration of the Being of God! No abstract arguments! No proofs *a priori!* Are these which have hitherto been so much insisted on by philosophers all fallacy, all sophism? Can we reach no farther in this subject than experience and probability? I will say not that this is betraying the cause of a Deity; but surely, by this affected candor, you give advantages to atheists which they never could obtain by the mere dint of argument and reasoning.

Philo: What I chiefly scruple in this subject, said *Philo*, is not so much that all religious arguments are by *Cleanthes* reduced to experience, as that they appear not be even the most certain and irrefragable of that inferior kind. That a stone will fall, that fire will burn, that the earth has solidity, we have observed a thousand and a thousand times; and when any new instance of this nature is presented, we draw without hesitation the accustomed inference. The exact similarity of the cases gives us a perfect assurance of a similar event, and a stronger evidence is never desired nor sought after. But wherever you depart, in the least, from the similarity of the cases, you diminish proportionably the evidence; and may at last bring it to a very weak *analogy*, which is confessedly liable to error and uncertainty. After having experienced the circulation of the blood in human creatures, we make no doubt that it takes place in *Titius* and *Maevius;* but from its circulation in frogs and fishes it is only a presumption, though a strong one, from analogy that it takes place in men and other animals. The analogical reasoning is much weaker when we infer the circulation of the sap in vegetables from our experience that the blood circulates in animals; and those who hastily followed that imperfect analogy are found, by more accurate experiments, to have been mistaken.

If we see a house, *Cleanthes,* we conclude, with the greatest certainty, that it had an architect or builder because this is precisely that species of effect which we have experienced to proceed from that species of cause. But surely you will not affirm that the universe bears such a resemblance to a house that we can with the same certainty infer a similar cause, or that the analogy is here entire and perfect. The dissimilitude is so striking that the utmost you can here pretend to is a guess, a conjecture, a presumption concerning a similar cause; and how that pretension will be received in the world, I leave you to consider.

Cleanthes: It would surely be very ill received, replied *Cleanthes;* and I should be deservedly blamed and detested did I allow that the proofs of a Deity amounted to no more than a guess or conjecture. But is the whole adjustment of means to ends in a house and in the universe so slight a resemblance? The economy of final causes? The order, proportion, and arrangement of every part? Steps of a stair are plainly contrived that human legs may use them in mounting; and this inference is certain and infallible. Human legs are also contrived for walking and mounting; and this inference, I allow, is not altogether so certain because of the dissimilarity which you remark; but does it, therefore, deserve the name only of presumption or conjecture?

Demea: Good God! cried *Demea*, interrupting him, where are we? Zealous defenders of religion allow that the proofs of a Deity fall short of perfect evidence! And you, *Philo*, on whose assistance I depended in proving the adorable mysteriousness of the Divine Nature, do you assent to all these extravagant opinions of *Cleanthes*? For what other name can I give them? or, why spare my censure when such principles are advanced, supported by such an authority, before so young a man as *Pamphilus*?

Philo: You seem not to apprehend, replied *Philo*, that I argue with *Cleanthes* in his own way, and, by showing him the dangerous consequences of his tenets, hope at last to reduce him to our opinion. But what sticks most with you, I observe, is the representation which *Cleanthes* has made of the argument *a posteriori;* and, finding that that argument is likely to escape your hold and vanish into air, you think it so disguised that you can scarcely believe it to be set in its true light. Now, however much I may dissent, in other respects, from the dangerous principle of *Cleanthes*, I must allow that he has fairly represented that argument, and I shall endeavor so to state the matter to you that you will entertain no further scruples with regard to it.

Were a man to abstract from everything which he knows or has seen, he would be altogether incapable, merely from his own ideas, to determine what kind of scene the universe must be, or to give the preference to one state or situation of things above another. For as nothing which he clearly conceives could be esteemed impossible or implying a contradiction, every chimera of his fancy would be upon an equal footing; nor could he assign any just reason why he adheres to one idea or system, and rejects the others which are equally possible.

Again, after he opens his eyes and contemplates the world as it really is, it would be impossible for him at first to assign the cause of any one event, much less of the whole of things, or of the universe. He might set his fancy a rambling, and she might bring him in an infinite variety of reports and representations. These would all be possible; but, being all equally possible, he would never of himself give a satisfactory account for his preferring one of them to the rest. Experience alone can point out to him the true cause of any phenomenon.

Now, according to this method of reasoning, *Demea*, it follows (and is, indeed, tacitly allowed by *Cleanthes* himself) that order, arrangement, or the adjustment of final causes, is not of itself any proof of design, but only so far as it has been experienced to proceed from that principle. For aught we can know *a priori*, matter may contain the source or spring of order originally within itself, as well as mind does; and there is no more difficulty in conceiving that the several elements, from an internal unknown cause, may fall into the most exquisite arrangement, than to conceive that their ideas, in the great universal mind, from a like internal unknown cause, fall into that arrangement. The equal possibility of both these suppositions is allowed. But, by experience, we find, according to *Cleanthes*, that there is a difference between them. Throw several pieces of steel together, without shape or form; they will never arrange themselves so as to compose a watch. Stone and mortar and wood, without an architect, never erect a house. But the ideas in a human mind, we see, by an unknown, inexplicable economy, arrange themselves so as to form the plan of a watch or house. Experience, therefore, proves that there is an original principle of order in mind, not in matter. From similar effects we infer similar causes. The adjustment of means to ends is alike in the universe, as in a machine of human contrivance. The causes, therefore, must be resembling.

I was from the beginning scandalized, I must own, with this resemblance which is asserted between the Deity and human creatures, and must conceive it to imply such a degradation of the Supreme Being as no sound theist could endure. With your assistance, therefore, *Demea*, I shall endeavor to defend what you justly call the adorable mysteriousness of the Divine Nature, and shall refute this reasoning of *Cleanthes*, provided he allows that I have made a fair representation of it.

When *Cleanthes* had assented, *Philo*, after a short pause, proceeded in the following manner.

That all inferences, *Cleanthes*, concerning fact are founded on experience, and that all experimental reasonings are founded on the supposition that similar causes prove similar effects, and similar effects similar causes, I shall not at present much dispute with you. But observe, I entreat you, with what extreme caution all just reasoners proceed in the transferring of experiments to similar cases. Unless the cases be exactly similar, they repose no perfect confidence in applying their past observation to any particular phenomenon. Every alteration of circumstances occasions a doubt concerning the event; and it requires new experiments to prove certainly that the new circumstances are of no moment or importance. A change in bulk, situation, arrangement, age, disposition of the air, or surrounding bodies; any of these particulars may be attended with the most unexpected consequences. And unless the objects be quite familiar to us, it is the highest temerity to expect with assurance, after any of these changes, an event similar to that which before fell under our observation. The slow and deliberate steps of philosophers here, if anywhere, are distinguished from the precipitate march of the vulgar, who, hurried on by the smallest similitude, are incapable of all discernment or consideration.

But can you think, *Cleanthes*, that your usual phlegm and philosophy have been preserved in so wide a step as you have taken when you compared to the universe houses, ships, furniture, machines; and, from their similarity in some circumstances, inferred a similarity in their causes? Thought, design, intelligence, such as we discover in men and other animals, is no more than one of the springs and principles of the universe, as well as heat or cold, attraction or repulsion, and a hundred others which fall under daily observation. It is an active cause by which some particular parts of nature, we find, produce alterations on other parts. But can a conclusion, with any propriety, be transferred from parts to the whole? Does not the great disproportion bar all comparison and inference? From observing the growth of a hair, can we learn anything concerning the generation of a man? Would the manner of a leaf's blowing, even though perfectly known, afford us any instruction concerning the vegetation of a tree?

But allowing that we were to take the *operations* of one part of nature upon another for the foundation of our judgment concerning the *origin* of the whole (which never can be admitted), yet why select so minute, so weak, so bounded a principle as the reason and design of animals is found to be upon this planet? What peculiar privilege has this little agitation of the brain which we call "thought", that we must thus make it the model of the whole universe? Our partiality in our own favor does indeed present it on all occasions, but sound philosophy ought carefully to guard against so natural an illusion.

So far from admitting, continued *Philo*, that the operations of a part can afford us any just conclusion concerning the origin of the whole, I will not allow any one part to form a rule for another part if the latter be very remote from the former. Is there any reasonable ground to conclude that the inhabitants of other planets possess thought, intelligence, reason, or anything similar to these faculties in men? When nature has so extremely diversified her manner of operation in this small globe, can we imagine that she incessantly copies herself throughout so immense a universe? And if thought, as we may well suppose, be confined merely to this narrow corner, and has even there so limited a sphere of action, with what propriety can we assign it for the original cause of all things? The narrow views of a peasant who makes his domestic economy the rule for the government of kingdoms is in comparison a pardonable sophism.

But were we ever so much assured that a thought and reason resembling the human were to be found throughout the whole universe, and were its activity elsewhere vastly greater and more commanding than it appears in this globe; yet I cannot see why the operations of a world constituted, arranged, adjusted, can with any propriety be extended to a world which is in its embryo-state, and is advancing towards that constitution and arrangement. By observation we know somewhat of the economy, action, and nourishment of a finished animal; but we must transfer with great caution that observation to the growth of a foetus in the womb, and still more to the formation of an animalcule in the loins of its male parent. Nature, we find, even from our limited experience, possesses an infinite number of springs and principles which incessantly discover themselves on every change of her position and situation. And what new and unknown principles would actuate her in so new and unknown a situation as that of the formation of a universe, we cannot, without the utmost temerity, pretend to determine.

A very small part of this great system, during a very short time, is very imperfectly discovered to us; and do we thence pronounce decisively concerning the origin of the whole?

Admirable conclusion! Stone, wood, brick, iron, brass, have not, at this time, in this minute globe of earth, an order or arrangement without human art and contrivance; therefore, the universe could not originally attain its order and arrangement without something similar to human art. But is a part of nature a rule for another part very wide of the former? Is it a rule for the whole? Is a very small part a rule for the universe? Is nature in one situation a certain rule for nature in another situation vastly different from the former?

And can you blame me, *Cleanthes*, if I here imitate the prudent reserve of *Simonides*, who, according to the noted story, being asked by *Hiero*, *What God was?* desired a day to think of it, and then two days more; and after that manner continually prolonged the term, without ever bringing in his definition or description? Could you even blame me if I had answered, at first, *that I did not know*, and was sensible that this subject lay vastly beyond the reach of my faculties? You might cry out skeptic and raillier, as much as you pleased; but, having found in so many other subjects much more familiar the imperfections and even contradictions of human reason, I never should expect any success from its feeble conjectures in a subject so sublime and so remote from the sphere of our observation. When two *species* of objects have always been observed to be conjoined together, I can *infer*, by custom, the existence of one wherever I *see* the existence of the other; and this I call an argument from experience. But how this argument can have place where the objects, as in the present case, are single, individual, without parallel or specific resemblance, may be difficult to explain. And will any man tell me with a serious countenance that an orderly universe must arise from some thought and art like the human because we have experience of it? To ascertain this reasoning it were requisite that we had experience of the origin of worlds; and it is not sufficient, surely, that we have seen ships and cities arise from human art and contrivance...

Philo was proceeding in this vehement manner, somewhat between jest and earnest, as it appeared to me, when he observed some signs of impatience in *Cleanthes*, and then immediately stopped short. **Cleanthes:** What I had to suggest, said *Cleanthes*, is only that you would not abuse terms, or make use of popular expressions to subvert philosophical reasonings. You know that the vulgar often distinguish reason from experience, even where the question relates only to matter of fact and existence, though it is found, where that *reason* is properly analyzed, that it is nothing but a species of experience. To prove by experience the origin of the universe from mind is not more contrary to common speech than to prove the motion of the earth from the same principle. And a caviller might raise all the same objections to the *Copernican* system which you have urged against my reasonings. Have you other earths, might he say, which you have seen to move? Have...

Philo: Yes! cried *Philo*, interrupting him, we have other earths. Is not the moon another earth, which we see to turn round its center? Is not Venus another earth, where we observe the same phenomenon? Are not the revolutions of the sun also a confirmation, from analogy, of the same theory? All the planets, are they not earths which revolve about the sun? Are not the satellites moons which move round Jupiter and Saturn, and along with these primary planets round the sun? These analogies and resemblances, with others which I have not mentioned, are the sole proofs of the *Copernican* system; and to you it belongs to consider whether you have any analogies of the same kind to support your theory.

In reality, *Cleanthes*, continued he, the modern system of astronomy is now so much received by all inquirers, and has become so essential a part even of our earliest education, that we are not commonly very scrupulous in examining the reasons upon which it is founded. It is now become a matter of mere curiosity to study the first writers on that subject who had the full force of prejudice to encounter, and were obliged to turn their arguments on every side in order to render them popular and convincing. But if we peruse *Galileo's* famous *Dialogues*[9] concerning the system of the world, we shall find that that great genius, one of the sublimest that ever existed, first bent all his endeavors to prove that there was no foundation for the distinction commonly made between elementary and celestial substances. The Schools, proceeding from the illusions of sense, had carried this distinction very far; and had established the latter substances to be ingenerable, incorruptible, unalterable, impassible; and had assigned all the opposite qualities to the former. But *Galileo*, beginning with the moon, proved its similarity in every particular to the earth: its convex figure, its natural darkness when not illuminated, its density, its distinction into solid and liquid, the variations of its phases, the mutual illuminations of the earth and moon, their mutual eclipses, the inequalities of the lunar surface, etc. After many instances of this kind, with regard to all the planets, men plainly saw that these bodies became proper objects of experience, and that the similarity of their nature enabled us to extend the same arguments and phenomena from one to the other.

In this cautious proceeding of the astronomers you may read your own condemnation, *Cleanthes*; or rather may see that the subject in which you are engaged exceeds all human reason and inquiry. Can you pretend to show any such similarity between the fabric of a house and the generation of a universe? Have you ever seen Nature in any such situation as resembles the first arrangement of the elements? Have worlds ever been formed under your eye, and have you had leisure to observe the whole progress of the phenomenon, from the first appearance of order to its final consummation? If you have, then cite your experience and deliver your theory.

9. [Galileo, *Dialogues on the Great World Systems* (1632).]

Part III

Cleanthes: How the most absurd argument, replied *Cleanthes*, in the hands of a man of ingenuity and invention, may acquire an air of probability! Are you not aware, *Philo*, that it became necessary for *Copernicus* and his first disciples to prove the similarity of the terrestrial and celestial matter because several philosophers, blinded by old systems and supported by some sensible appearances, had denied this similarity; but that it is by no means necessary that theists should prove the similarity of the works of nature to those of art, because this similarity is self-evident and undeniable? The same matter, a like form; what more is requisite to show an analogy between their causes, and to ascertain the origin of all things from a divine purpose and intention? Your objections, I must freely tell you, are no better than the abstruse cavils of those philosophers who denied motion, and ought to be refuted in the same manner—by illustrations, examples, and instances rather than by serious argument and philosophy.[10]

Suppose, therefore, that an articulate voice were heard in the clouds, much louder and more melodious than any which human art could ever reach; suppose that this voice were extended in the same instant over all nations and spoke to each nation in its own language and dialect; suppose that the words delivered not only contain a just sense and meaning, but convey some instruction altogether worthy of a benevolent Being superior to mankind—could you possibly hesitate a moment concerning the cause of this voice, and must you not instantly ascribe it to some design or purpose? Yet I cannot see but all the same objections (if they merit that appellation) which lie against the system of theism may also be produced against this inference.

Might you not say that all conclusions concerning fact were

10. [Diogenes was supposed to have listened to Zeno's arguments denying that motion really occurs. Diogenes got up and walked around, and claimed that was sufficient refutation of Zeno's view.]

founded on experience; that, when we hear an articulate voice in the dark and thence infer a man, it is only the resemblance of the effects which leads us to conclude that there is a like resemblance in the cause; but that this extraordinary voice, by its loudness, extent, and flexibility to all languages, bears so little analogy to any human voice that we have no reason to suppose any analogy in their causes; and, consequently, that a rational, wise, coherent speech proceeded, you know not whence, from some accidental whistling of the winds, not from any divine reason or intelligence? You see clearly your own objections in these cavils; and I hope too, you see clearly that they cannot possibly have more force in the one case than in the other.

But to bring the case still nearer the present one of the universe, I shall make two suppositions which imply not any absurdity or impossibility. Suppose that there is a natural, universal, invariable language, common to every individual of human race, and that books are natural productions which perpetuate themselves in the same manner with animals and vegetables, by descent and propagation. Several expressions of our passions contain a universal language: All brute animals have a natural speech, which, however limited, is very intelligible to their own species. And as there are infinitely fewer parts and less contrivance in the finest composition of eloquence than in the coarsest organized body, the propagation of an *Iliad* or *Aeneid* is an easier supposition than that of any plant or animal.

Suppose, therefore, that you enter into your library thus peopled by natural volumes containing the most refined reason and most exquisite beauty. Could you possibly open one of them and doubt that its original cause bore the strongest analogy to mind and intelligence? When it reasons and discourses; when it expostulates, argues, and enforces its views and topics; when it applies sometimes to the pure intellect, sometimes to the affections; when it collects, disposes, and adorns every consideration suited to the subject; could you persist in asserting that all this, at the bottom, had really no meaning, and that the first formation of this volume in the loins of its original parent proceeded not from thought and design? Your obstinacy, I know, reaches not that degree of firmness; even your skeptical play and wantonness would be abashed at so glaring an absurdity.

But if there be any difference, *Philo*, between this supposed case and the real one of the universe, it is all to the advantage of the latter. The anatomy of an animal affords many stronger instances of design than the perusal of *Livy* or *Tacitus;* and any objection which you start in the former case, by carrying me back to so unusual and extraordinary a scene as the first formation of worlds, the same objection has place on the supposition of our vegetating library. Choose, then, your party, *Philo,* without ambiguity or evasion; assert either that a rational volume is no proof of a rational cause or admit of a similar cause to all the works of nature.

Let me here observe, too, continued *Cleanthes,* that this religious argument, instead of being weakened by that skepticism so much affected by you, rather acquires force from it and becomes more firm and undisputed. To exclude all argument or reasoning of every kind is either affectation or madness. The declared profession of every reasonable skeptic is only to reject abstruse, remote, and refined arguments; to adhere to common sense and the plain instincts of nature; and to assent, wherever any reasons strike him with so full a force that he cannot, without the greatest violence, prevent it. Now the arguments for natural religion are plainly of this kind; and nothing but the most perverse, obstinate metaphysics can reject them. Consider, anatomize the eye; survey its structure and contrivance, and tell me, from your own feeling, if the idea of a contriver does not immediately flow in upon you with a force like that of sensation. The most obvious conclusion, surely, is in favor of design; and it requires time, reflection, and study, to summon up those frivolous though abstruse objections which can support infidelity. Who can behold the male and female of each species, the correspondence of their parts and instincts, their passions and whole course of life before and after generation, but must be sensible that the propagation of the species is intended by nature? Millions and millions of such instances present themselves through every part of the universe, and no language can convey a more intelligible, irresistible meaning than the curious adjustment of final causes. To what degree, therefore, of blind dogmatism must one have attained to reject such natural and such convincing arguments?

Some beauties in writing we may meet with which seem contrary to rules, and which gain the affections and animate the imagination in opposition to all the precepts of criticism and to the authority of the established masters of art. And if the argument for theism be, as you pretend, contradictory to the principles of logic, its universal, its irresistible influence proves clearly that there may be arguments of a like irregular nature. Whatever cavils may be urged, an orderly world, as well as a coherent, articulate speech, will still be received as an incontestable proof of design and intention.

It sometimes happens, I own, that the religious arguments have not their due influence on an ignorant savage and barbarian; not because they are obscure and difficult, but because he never asks himself any question with regard to them. Whence arises the curious structure of an animal? From the copulation of its parents. And these whence? From *their* parents? A few removes set the objects at such a distance that to him they are lost in darkness and confusion; nor is he actuated by any curiosity to trace them farther. But this is neither dogmatism nor skepticism, but stupidity: a state of mind very different from your sifting, inquisitive disposition, my ingenious friend. You can trace causes from effects; you can compare the most distant and remote objects; and your greatest errors proceed not from barrenness of thought and invention, but from too luxuriant a fertility which suppresses your natural good sense by a profusion of unnecessary scruples and objections.

Pamphilus: Here I could observe, *Hermippus*, that *Philo* was a little embarrassed and confounded. But, while he hesitated in delivering an answer, luckily for him, *Demea* broke in upon the discourse and saved his countenance.

Demea: Your instance, *Cleanthes*, said he, drawn from books and language, being familiar, has, I confess, so much more force on that account; but is there not some danger, too, in this very circumstance, and may it not render us presumptuous, by making us imagine we comprehend the Deity and have some adequate idea of his nature and attributes? When I read a volume, I enter into the mind and intention of the author; I become him, in a manner, for the instant, and have an immediate feeling and conception of those ideas which revolved in his imagination while employed in that composition. But so near an approach we never surely can make to the Deity. His ways are not our ways. His attributes are perfect but incomprehensible. And this volume of nature contains a great and inexplicable riddle, more than any intelligible discourse or reasoning.

The ancient *Platonists*, you know, were the most religious and devout of all the pagan philosophers; yet many of them, particularly *Plotinus*,[11] expressly declare that intellect or understanding is not to be ascribed to the Deity, and that our most perfect worship of

11. [Plotinus, A.D. 205–270, the leading figure in the ancient neoplatonic school of philosophy]

him consists, not in acts of veneration, reverence, gratitude, or love, but in a certain mysterious self-annihilation or total extinction of all our faculties. These ideas are, perhaps, too far stretched; but still it must be acknowledged that, by representing the Deity as so intelligible and comprehensible, and so similar to a human mind, we are guilty of the grossest and most narrow partiality, and make ourselves the model of the whole universe.

All the *sentiments* of the human mind, gratitude, resentment, love, friendship, approbation, blame, pity, emulation, envy, have a plain reference to the state and situation of man, and are calculated for preserving the existence and promoting the activity of such a being in such circumstances. It seems, therefore, unreasonable to transfer such sentiments to a supreme existence or to suppose him actuated by them; and the phenomena, besides, of the universe will not support us in such a theory. All our *ideas* derived from the senses are confessedly false and illusive, and cannot therefore be supposed to have place in a Supreme Intelligence. And as the ideas of internal sentiment, added to those of the external senses, compose the whole furniture of human understanding, we may conclude that none of the *materials* of thought are in any respect similar in the human and in the Divine Intelligence. Now, as to the *manner* of thinking, how can we make any comparison between them or suppose them anywise resembling? Our thought is fluctuating, uncertain, fleeting, successive, and compounded; and were we to remove these circumstances, we absolutely annihilate its essence, and it would in such a case be an abuse of terms to apply to it the name of thought or reason. At least, if it appear more pious and respectful (as it really is) still to retain these terms when we mention the Supreme Being, we ought to acknowledge that their meaning, in that case, is totally incomprehensible; and that the infirmities of our nature do not permit us to reach any ideas which in the least correspond to the ineffable sublimity of the Divine Attributes.

Part IV

Cleanthes: It seems strange to me, said *Cleanthes,* that you, *Demea,* who are so sincere in the cause of religion, should still maintain the mysterious, incomprehensible nature of the Deity, and should insist so strenuously that he has no manner of likeness or resemblance to human creatures. The Deity, I can readily allow, possesses many powers and attributes of which we can have no comprehension. But, if our ideas, so far as they go, be not just and adequate and correspondent to his real nature, I know not what there is in this subject worth insisting on. Is the name, without any meaning, of such mighty importance? Or how do you *mystics,* who maintain the absolute incomprehensibility of the Deity, differ from skeptics or atheists, who assert that the first cause of all is unknown and unintelligible? Their temerity must be very great if, after rejecting the production by a mind; I mean a mind resembling the human (for I know of no other), they pretend to assign, with certainty, any other specific intelligible cause; and their conscience must be very scrupulous, indeed, if they refuse to call the universal unknown cause a God or Deity, and to bestow on him as many sublime eulogies and unmeaning epithets as you shall please to require of them.

Demea: Who could imagine, replied *Demea,* that *Cleanthes,* the calm philosophical *Cleanthes,* would attempt to refute his antagonists by affixing a nickname to them; and, like the common bigots and inquisitors of the age, have recourse to invective and declamation instead of reasoning? Or does he not perceive that these topics are easily retorted, and that *anthropomorphite* is an appellation as invidious, and implies as dangerous consequences, as the epithet of *mystic* with which he has honored us? In reality, *Cleanthes,* consider what it is you assert when you represent the Deity as similar to a human mind and understanding. What is the soul of man? A composition of various faculties, passions, sentiments, ideas; united, indeed, into one self or person, but still distinct from each other.

When it reasons, the ideas which are the parts of its discourse arrange themselves in a certain form or order, which is not preserved entire for a moment, but immediately gives place to another arrangement. New opinions, new passions, new affections, new feelings arise which continually diversify the mental scene and produce in it the greatest variety and most rapid succession imaginable. How is this compatible with that perfect immutability and simplicity which all true theists ascribe to the Deity? By the same act, say they, he sees past, present, and future; his love and hatred, his mercy and justice, are one individual operation: He is entire in every point of space, and complete in every instant of duration. No succession, no change, no acquisition, no diminution. What he is implies not in it any shadow of distinction or diversity. And what he is this moment he ever has been and ever will be, without any new judgment, sentiment, or operation. He stands fixed in one simple, perfect state; nor can you ever say, with any propriety, that this act of his is different from that other, or that this judgment or idea has been lately formed and will give place, by succession, to any different judgment or idea.

Cleanthes: I can readily allow, said *Cleanthes*, that those who maintain the perfect simplicity of the Supreme Being, to the extent in which you have explained it, are complete *mystics*, and chargeable with all the consequences which I have drawn from their opinion. They are, in a word, *atheists*, without knowing it. For though it be allowed that the Deity possesses attributes of which we have no comprehension, yet ought we never to ascribe to him any attributes which are absolutely incompatible with that intelligent nature essential to him. A mind whose acts and sentiments and ideas are not distinct and successive, one that is wholly simple and totally immutable, is a mind which has no thought, no reason, no will, no sentiment, no love, no hatred; or, in a word, is no mind at all. It is an abuse of terms to give it that appellation, and we may as well speak of limited extension without figure, or of number without composition.

Philo: Pray consider, said *Philo*, whom you are at present inveighing against. You are honoring with the appellation of *atheist* all the sound, orthodox divines, almost, who have treated of this subject; and you will at last be, yourself, found, according to your reckoning, the only sound theist in the world. But if idolaters be atheists, as, I think, may justly be asserted, and *Christian* theologians the same, what becomes of the argument, so much celebrated, derived from the universal consent of mankind?[12]

But, because I know you are not much swayed by names and authorities, I shall endeavor to show you, a little more distinctly, the inconveniences of that anthropomorphism which you have embraced, and shall prove that there is no ground to suppose a plan of the world to be formed in the Divine Mind, consisting of distinct ideas, differently arranged, in the same manner as an architect forms in his head the plan of a house which he intends to execute.

It is not easy, I own, to see what is gained by this supposition, whether we judge of the matter by *reason* or by *experience*. We are still obliged to mount higher in order to find the cause of this cause which you had assigned as satisfactory and conclusive.

If *reason* (I mean abstract reason derived from inquiries a priori) be not alike mute with regard to all questions concerning cause and effect, this sentence at least it will venture to pronounce: that a mental world or universe of ideas requires a cause as much as does a material world or universe of objects; and, if similar in its arrangement, must require a similar cause. For what is there in this subject which should occasion a different conclusion or inference? In an abstract view, they are entirely alike; and no difficulty attends the one supposition which is not common to both of them.

Again, when we will needs force *experience* to pronounce some sentence, even on these subjects which lie beyond her sphere; neither can she perceive any material difference in this particular between these two kinds of worlds, but finds them to be governed by similar principles, and to depend upon an equal variety of causes in their operations. We have specimens in miniature of both of them. Our own mind resembles the one; a vegetable or animal body the other. Let experience, therefore judge from these samples. Nothing seems more delicate, with regard to its causes, than thought; and as these causes never operate in two persons after the same manner, so we never find two persons who think exactly alike. Nor indeed does the same person think exactly alike at any two different periods of time. A difference of age, of the disposition of his body, of weather, of food, of company, of books, of passions; any of these particulars, or others more minute, are sufficient to alter the curious machinery of thought and communicate to it very different movements and operations. As far as we can judge, vegetables and animal bodies are not more delicate in their motions, nor depend

12. [An argument that had been popularized in the seventeenth century by Herbert of Cherbury and Hugo Grotius.]

upon a greater variety or more curious adjustment of springs and principles.

How, therefore, shall we satisfy ourselves concerning the cause of that Being whom you suppose the Author of Nature, or, according to your system of anthropomorphism, the Ideal World into which you trace the material? Have we not the same reason to trace that ideal world into another ideal world or new intelligent principle? But if we stop and go no farther, why go so far? Why not stop at the material world? How can we satisfy ourselves without going on *in infinitum*? And, after all, what satisfaction is there in that infinite progression? Let us remember the story of the Indian philosopher and his elephant.[13] It was never more applicable than to the present subject. If the material world rests upon a similar ideal world, this ideal world must rest upon some other, and so on without end. It were better, therefore, never to look beyond the present material world. By supposing it to contain the principle of its order within itself, we really assert it to be God; and the sooner we arrive at that Divine Being, so much the better. When you go one step beyond the mundane system, you only excite an inquisitive humor which it is impossible ever to satisfy.

To say that the different ideas which compose the reason of the Supreme Being fall into order of themselves and by their own nature is really to talk without any precise meaning. If it has a meaning, I would fain know why it is not as good sense to say that the parts of the material world fall into order of themselves and by their own nature? Can the one opinion be intelligible, while the other is not so?

We have, indeed, experience of ideas which fall into order of themselves and without any *known* cause. But, I am sure, we have a much larger experience of matter which does the same, as in all instances of generation and vegetation where the accurate analysis of the cause exceeds all human comprehension. We have also experience of particular systems of thought and of matter which have no order; of the first in madness, of the second in corruption. Why, then, should we think that order is more essential to one than the other? And if it requires a cause in both, what do we gain by your system, in tracing the universe of objects into a similar universe of ideas? The first step which we make leads us on forever. It were, therefore, wise in us to limit all our inquiries to the present world,

---

13. [This appears in John Locke, *An Essay Concerning Human Understanding*, Book II, chap XIII, sec. 2. The Indian philosopher said the world was resting on the back of an elephant; the elephant on the back of a great tortoise; the great tortoise on the back of he knew not what.]

without looking farther. No satisfaction can ever be attained by these speculations which so far exceed the narrow bounds of human understanding.

It was usual with the *Peripatetics*,[14] you know, *Cleanthes*, when the cause of any phenomenon was demanded, to have recourse to their *faculties* or *occult qualities*, and to say, for instance, that bread nourished by its nutritive faculty, and senna purged by its purgative. But it has been discovered that this subterfuge was nothing but the disguise of ignorance, and that these philosophers, though less ingenuous, really said the same thing with the skeptics or the vulgar who fairly confessed that they knew not the cause of these phenomena. In like manner, when it is asked, what cause produces order in the ideas of the Supreme Being, can any other reason be assigned by you, anthropomorphites, than that it is a *rational* faculty, and that such is the nature of the Deity? But why a similar answer will not be equally satisfactory in accounting for the order of the world, without having recourse to any such intelligent creator as you insist on, may be difficult to determine. It is only to say that *such* is the nature of material objects, and that they are all originally possessed of a *faculty* of order and proportion. These are only more learned and elaborate ways of confessing our ignorance; nor has the one hypothesis any real advantage above the other, except in its greater conformity to vulgar prejudices.

Cleanthes: You have displayed this argument with great emphasis, replied *Cleanthes:* You seem not sensible how easy it is to answer it. Even in common life, if I assign a cause for any event, is it any objection, *Philo*, that I cannot assign the cause of that cause, and answer every new question which may incessantly be started? And what philosophers could possibly submit to so rigid a rule? Philosophers who confess ultimate causes to be totally unknown, and are sensible that the most refined principles into which they trace the phenomena are still to them as inexplicable as these phenomena themselves are to the vulgar. The order and arrangement of Nature, the curious adjustment of final causes, the plain use and intention of every part and organ; all these bespeak in the clearest language an intelligent cause or author. The heavens and the earth join in the same testimony: The whole chorus of Nature raises one hymn to the praises of its Creator: You alone, or almost alone, disturb this general harmony. You start abstruse doubts, cavils, and objections; you ask me what is the cause of this cause? I know not; I care not; that concerns not me. I have found a Deity;

14. [The followers of Aristotle.]

and here I stop my inquiry. Let those go farther who are wiser or more enterprising.

Philo: I pretend to be neither, replied *Philo;* and for that very reason I should never, perhaps, have attempted to go so far, especially when I am sensible that I must at last be contented to sit down with the same answer which, without further trouble, might have satisfied me from the beginning. If I am still to remain in utter ignorance of causes and can absolutely give an explication of nothing, I shall never esteem it any advantage to shove off for a moment a difficulty which you acknowledge must immediately, in its full force, recur upon me. Naturalists, indeed, very justly explain particular effects by more general causes, though these general causes themselves should remain in the end totally inexplicable; but they never surely thought it satisfactory to explain a particular effect by a particular cause which was no more to be accounted for than the effect itself. An ideal system, arranged of itself, without a precedent design, is not a whit more explicable than a material one which attains its order in a like manner; nor is there any more difficulty in the latter supposition than in the former.

Part V

Philo: But to show you still more inconveniences, continued *Philo*, in your anthropomorphism, please to take a new survey of your principles. *Like effects prove like causes.* This is the experimental argument; and this, you say too, is the sole theological argument. Now it is certain that the liker the effects are which are seen and the liker the causes which are inferred, the stronger is the argument. Every departure on either side diminishes the probability and renders the experiment less conclusive. You cannot doubt of the principle; neither ought you to reject its consequences.

All the new discoveries in astronomy which prove the immense grandeur and magnificence of the works of nature are so many additional arguments for a Deity, according to the true system of theism; but, according to your hypothesis of experimental theism, they become so many objections, by removing the effect still farther from all resemblance to the effects of human art and contrivance. For if *Lucretius,* even following the old system of the world, could exclaim:

> Who is strong enough to rule the sum, who to hold in hand and control the mighty bridle of the unfathomable deep? who to turn about all the heavens at one time, and warm the fruitful worlds with ethereal fires, or to be present in all places and at all times.[15]

If Tully[16] esteemed this reasoning so natural as to put it into the mouth of his Epicurean:

> What power of mental vision enabled your master Plato to descry the vast and elaborate architectural process which, as he makes out, the deity adopted in building the structure of the universe?

15. [*On the Nature of Things,* II, 1096–1099 (trans. by W.D. Rouse).]

16. [Tully was a common name for the Roman lawyer and philosopher, Marcus Tullius Cicero, 106–43 B.C.]

What method of engineering was employed? What tools and levers and derricks? What agents carried out so vast an understanding? And how were air, fire, water, and earth enabled to obey and execute the will of the architect?[17]

If this argument, I say, had any force in former ages, how much greater must it have at present when the bounds of nature are so infinitely enlarged and such a magnificent scene is opened to us? It is still more unreasonable to form our idea of so unlimited a cause from our experience of the narrow productions of human design and invention.

The discoveries by microscopes, as they open a new universe in miniature, are still objections, according to you; arguments, according to me. The farther we push our researches of this kind, we are still led to infer the universal cause of all to be vastly different from mankind, or from any object of human experience and observation.

And what say you to the discoveries in anatomy, chemistry, botany?... **Cleanthes:** These surely are no objections, replied *Cleanthes;* they only discover new instances of art and contrivance. It is still the image of mind reflected on us from innumerable objects. **Philo:** Add a mind *like the human,* said *Philo.* **Cleanthes:** I know of no other, replied *Cleanthes.* **Philo:** And the liker, the better, insisted *Philo.* **Cleanthes:** To be sure, said *Cleanthes.*

Philo: Now, *Cleanthes,* said *Philo,* with an air of alacrity and triumph, mark the consequences. *First,* by this method of reasoning you renounce all claim to infinity in any of the attributes of the Deity. For, as the cause ought only to be proportioned to the effect, and the effect, so far as it falls under our cognizance, is not infinite: What pretensions have we, upon your suppositions, to ascribe that attribute to the Divine Being? You will still insist that, by removing him so much from all similarity to human creatures, we give in to the most arbitrary hypothesis, and at the same time weaken all proofs of his existence.

Secondly, you have no reason, on your theory, for ascribing perfection to the Deity, even in his finite capacity; or for supposing him free from every error, mistake, or incoherence, in his undertakings. There are many inexplicable difficulties in the works of Nature which, if we allow a perfect author to be proved *a priori,* are easily

17. [Cicero, *The Nature of the Gods,* I, viii, 19 (trans. by H. Rackham).]

solved, and become only seeming difficulties from the narrow capacity of man, who cannot trace infinite relations. But according to your method of reasoning, these difficulties become all real; and, perhaps, will be insisted on as new instances of likeness to human art and contrivance. At least, you must acknowledge that it is impossible for us to tell, from our limited views, whether this system contains any great faults or deserves any considerable praise if compared to other possible and even real systems. Could a peasant, if the *Aeneid* were read to him, pronounce that poem to be absolutely faultless, or even assign to it its proper rank among the productions of human wit, he who had never seen any other production?

But were this world ever so perfect a production, it must still remain uncertain whether all the excellences of the work can justly be ascribed to the workman. If we survey a ship, what an exalted idea must we form of the ingenuity of the carpenter who framed so complicated, useful, and beautiful a machine? And what surprise must we feel when we find him a stupid mechanic who imitated others, and copied an art which, through a long succession of ages, after multiplied trials, mistakes, corrections, deliberations, and controversies, had been gradually improving? Many worlds might have been botched and bungled, throughout an eternity, ere this system was struck out; much labor lost; many fruitless trials made; and a slow but continued improvement carried on during infinite ages in the art of world-making. In such subjects, who can determine where the truth, nay, who can conjecture where the probability lies, amidst a great number of hypotheses which may be proposed, and a still greater which may be imagined?

And what shadow of an argument, continued Philo, can you produce from your hypothesis to prove the unity of the Deity? A great number of men join in building a house or ship, in rearing a city, in framing a commonwealth; why may not several deities combine in contriving and framing a world? This is only so much greater similarity to human affairs. By sharing the work among several, we may so much further limit the attributes of each, and get rid of that extensive power and knowledge which must be supposed in one deity, and which, according to you, can only serve to weaken the proof of his existence. And if such foolish, such vicious creatures as man can yet often unite in framing and executing one plan, how much more those deities or demons, whom we may suppose several degrees more perfect?

To multiply causes without necessity is indeed contrary to true philosophy, but this principle applies not to the present case. Were one deity antecedently proved by your theory who were possessed of every attribute requisite to the production of the universe, it would be needless, I own (though not absurd), to suppose any other deity existent. But while it is still a question whether all these attributes are united in one subject or dispersed among several independent beings; by what phenomena in nature can we pretend to decide the controversy? Where we see a body raised in a scale, we are sure that there is in the opposite scale, however concealed from sight, some counterpoising weight equal to it; but it is still allowed to doubt whether that weight be an aggregate of several distinct bodies or one uniform united mass. And if the weight requisite very much exceeds anything which we have ever seen conjoined in any single body, the former supposition becomes still more probable and natural. An intelligent being of such vast power and capacity as is necessary to produce the universe, or, to speak in the language of ancient philosophy, so prodigious an animal, exceeds all analogy and even comprehension.

But further, *Cleanthes*, men are mortal, and renew their species by generation; and this is common to all living creatures. The two great sexes of male and female, says *Milton*, animate the world. Why must this circumstance, so universal, so essential, be excluded from those numerous and limited deities? Behold, then, the theogeny of ancient times brought back upon us.

And why not become a perfect anthropomorphite? Why not assert the deity or deities to be corporeal, and to have eyes, a nose, mouth, ears, etc.? *Epicurus* maintained that no man had ever seen reason but in a human figure; therefore, the gods must have a human figure. And this argument, which is deservedly so much ridiculed by *Cicero*, becomes, according to you, solid and philosophical.

In a word, *Cleanthes*, a man who follows your hypothesis is able, perhaps, to assert or conjecture that the universe sometime arose from something like design: But beyond that position he cannot ascertain one single circumstance, and is left afterwards to fix every point of his theology by the utmost license of fancy and hypothesis. This world, for aught he knows, is very faulty and imperfect, compared to a superior standard; and was only the first rude essay of some infant deity who afterwards abandoned it, ashamed of his lame performance: It is the work only of some dependent, inferior deity, and is the object of derision to his superiors: It is the production of old age and dotage in some superannuated deity; and ever since his death has run on at adventures, from the first impulse and active force which it received from him. . . .You justly give signs of horror, *Demea*, at these strange suppositions; but these, and a thousand more of the same kind, are *Cleanthes'* suppositions, not mine. From the moment the attributes of the Deity are supposed finite, all these have place. And I cannot, for my part, think that so wild and unsettled a system of theology is, in any respect, preferable to none at all.

Cleanthes: These suppositions I absolutely disown, cried *Cleanthes:* They strike me, however, with no horror, especially when proposed in that rambling way in which they drop from you. On the contrary, they give me pleasure when I see that, by the utmost indulgence of your imagination, you never get rid of the hypothesis of design in the universe, but are obliged at every turn to have recourse to it. To this concession I adhere steadily; and this I regard as a sufficient foundation for religion.

Part VI

Demea: It must be a slight fabric, indeed, said *Demea*, which can be erected on so tottering a foundation. While we are uncertain whether there is one deity or many, whether the deity or deities, to whom we owe our existence, be perfect or imperfect, subordinate or supreme, dead or alive; what trust or confidence can we repose in them? What devotion or worship address to them? What veneration or obedience pay them? To all the purposes of life the theory of religion becomes altogether useless; and even with regard to speculative consequences its uncertainty, according to you, must render it totally precarious and unsatisfactory.

Philo: To render it still more unsatisfactory, said *Philo*, there occurs to me another hypothesis which must acquire an air of probability from the method of reasoning so much insisted on by *Cleanthes*. That like effects arise from like causes: This principle he supposes the foundation of all religion. But there is another principle of the same kind, no less certain and derived from the same source of experience; that, where several known circumstances are *observed* to be similar, the unknown will also be *found* similar. Thus, if we see the limbs of a human body, we conclude that it is also attended with a human head, though hid from us. Thus, if we see, through a chink in a wall, a small part of the sun, we conclude that were the wall removed we should see the whole body. In short, this method of reasoning is so obvious and familiar that no scruple can ever be made with regard to its solidity.

Now, if we survey the universe, so far it falls under our knowledge, it bears a great resemblance to an animal or organized body, and seems actuated with a like principle of life and motion. A continual circulation of matter in it produces no disorder; a continual waste in every part is incessantly repaired: The closest sympathy is perceived throughout the entire system: And each part or member, in performing its proper offices, operates both to its own preservation and to that of the whole. The world, therefore, I infer, is an animal; and the Deity is the *Soul* of the world, actuating it, and actuated by it.

You have too much learning, *Cleanthes*, to be at all surprised at this opinion which, you know, was maintained by almost all the theists of antiquity, and chiefly prevails in their discourses and reasonings. For though sometimes the ancient philosophers reason from final causes, as if they thought the world the workmanship of God, yet it appears rather their favorite notion to consider it as his body whose organization renders it subservient to him. And it must be confessed that, as the universe resembles more a human body than it does the works of human art and contrivance, if our limited analogy could ever, with any propriety, be extended to the whole of nature, the inference seems juster in favor of the ancient than the modern theory.

There are many other advantages, too, in the former theory which recommended it to the ancient theologians. Nothing more repugnant to all their notions, because nothing more repugnant to common experience, than mind without body; a mere spiritual substance which fell not under their senses nor comprehension, and of which they had not observed one single instance throughout all nature. Mind and body they knew because they felt both; an order, arrangement, organization, or internal machinery, in both they likewise knew, after the same manner: And it could not but seem reasonable to transfer this experience to the universe, and to suppose the divine mind and body to be also coeval and to have, both of them, order and arrangement naturally inherent in them and inseparable from them.

Here, therefore, is a new species of *Anthropomorphism, Cleanthes,* on which you may deliberate; and a theory which seems not liable to any considerable difficulties. You are too much superior, surely, to *systematical prejudices* to find any more difficulty in supposing an animal body to be, originally, of itself or from unknown causes, possessed of order and organization, than in supposing a similar order to belong to mind. But the *vulgar prejudice* that body and mind ought always to accompany each other ought not, one should think, to be entirely neglected; since it is founded on *vulgar experience*, the only guide which you profess to follow in all these theological inquiries. And if you assert that our limited experience is an unequal standard by which to judge of the unlimited extent of nature, you entirely abandon your own hypothesis and must thenceforward adopt our mysticism, as you call it, and admit of the absolute incomprehensibility of the Divine Nature.

Cleanthes: This theory, I own, replied *Cleanthes,* has never before occurred to me, though a pretty natural one; and I cannot readily, upon so short an examination and reflection, deliver any opinion with regard to it. **Philo:** You are very scrupulous, indeed, said *Philo:* Were I to examine any system of yours, I should not have acted with half that caution and reserve, in starting objections and difficulties to it. However, if anything occur to you, you will oblige us by proposing it.

Cleanthes: Why then, replied *Cleanthes,* it seems to me that, though the world does, in many circumstances, resemble an animal body, yet is the analogy also defective in many circumstances the most material: No organs of sense; no seat of thought or reason; no one precise origin of motion and action. In short, it seems to bear a stronger resemblance to a vegetable than to an animal, and your inference would be so far inconclusive in favor of the soul of the world.

But, in the next place, your theory seems to imply the eternity of the world; and that is a principle which, I think, can be refuted by the strongest reasons and probabilities. I shall suggest an argument to this purpose which, I believe, has not been insisted on by any writer. Those who reason from the late origin of arts and sciences, though their inference wants not force, may perhaps be refuted by considerations derived from the nature of human society, which is in continual revolution between ignorance and knowledge, liberty and slavery, riches and poverty; so that it is impossible for us, from our limited experience, to foretell with assurance what events may or may not be expected. Ancient learning and history seem to have been in great danger of entirely perishing after the inundation of the barbarous nations; and had these convulsions continued a little longer, or been a little more violent, we should not probably have now known what passed in the world a few centuries before us. Nay, were it not for the superstition of the popes, who preserved a little jargon of Latin in order to support the appearance of an ancient and universal church, that tongue must have been utterly lost: In which case the Western world, being totally barbarous, would not have been in a fit disposition for receiving the Greek language and learning, which was conveyed to them after the sacking of Constantinople. When learning and books had been extinguished, even the mechanical arts would have fallen considerable to decay; and it is easily imagined that fable or tradition might ascribe to them a much later origin than the true one. This vulgar argument, therefore, against the eternity of the world seems a little precarious.

But here appears to be the foundation of a better argument. *Lucullus* was the first that brought cherry-trees from Asia to Europe; though that tree thrives so well in many European climates that it grows in the woods without any culture. Is it possible that, throughout a whole eternity, no European had ever passed into Asia and thought of transplanting so delicious a fruit into his own country? Or if the tree was once transplanted and propagated, how could it ever afterwards perish? Empires may rise and fall; liberty and slavery succeed alternately; ignorance and knowledge give place to each other; but the cherry-tree will still remain in the woods of Greece, Spain, and Italy, and will never be affected by the revolutions of human society.

It is not two thousand years since vines were transplanted into France, though there is no climate in the world more favorable to them. It is not three centuries since horses, cows, sheep, swine, dogs, corn, were known in America. Is it possible that during the revolutions of a whole eternity there never arose a *Columbus* who might open the communication between Europe and that continent? We may as well imagine that all men would wear stockings for ten thousand years, and never have the sense to think of garters to tie them. All these seem convincing proofs of the youth or rather infancy of the world, as being founded on the operation of principles more constant and steady than those by which human society is governed and directed. Nothing less than a total convulsion of the elements will ever destroy all the European animals and vegetables which are now to be found in the Western world.

Philo: And what argument have you against such convulsions? replied *Philo*. Strong and almost incontestable proofs may be traced over the whole earth that every part of this globe has continued for many ages entirely covered with water. And though order were supposed inseparable from matter, and inherent in it; yet may matter be susceptible of many and great revolutions, through the endless periods of eternal duration. The incessant changes to which every part of it is subject seem to intimate some such general transformations; though, at the same time, it is observable that all the changes and corruptions of which we have ever had experience are but passages from one state of order to another; nor can matter ever rest in total deformity and confusion. What we see in the parts, we may infer in the whole; at least, that is the method of reasoning on which you rest your whole theory. And were I obliged to defend any particular system of this nature, (which I never willingly should do), I esteem none more plausible than that which ascribes an eternal, inherent principle of order to the world, though attended with great and continual revolutions and alterations. This at once solves all difficulties; and if the solution, by being so general, is not entirely complete and satisfactory, it is at least a theory that we must sooner or later have recourse to, whatever system we embrace. How could things have been as they are, were there not an original inherent principle of order somewhere, in thought or in matter? And it is very indifferent to which of these we give the preference. Chance has no place, on any hypothesis, skeptical or religious. Everything is surely governed by steady, inviolable laws. And were the inmost essence of things laid open to us, we should then discover a scene of which, at present, we can have no idea. Instead of admiring the order of natural beings, we should clearly see that it was absolutely impossible for them, in the smallest article, ever to admit of any other disposition.

Were anyone inclined to revive the ancient pagan theology which maintained, as we learn from *Hesiod*, that this globe was governed by 30,000 deities, who arose from the unknown powers of nature, you would naturally object, *Cleanthes*, that nothing is gained by this hypothesis; and that it is as easy to suppose all men and animals, beings more numerous but less perfect, to have sprung immediately from a like origin. Push the same inference a step further, and you will find a numerous society of deities as explicable as one universal deity who possesses within himself the powers and perfections of the whole society. All these systems, then, of skepticism, polytheism, and theism, you must allow, on your principles, to be on a like footing, and that no one of them has any advantage over the others. You may thence learn the fallacy of your principles.

Part VII

Philo: But here, continued *Philo*, in examining the ancient system of the soul of the world there strikes me, all on a sudden, a new idea which, if just, must go near to subvert all your reasoning, and destroy even your first inferences on which you repose such confidence. If the universe bears a greater likeness to animal bodies and to vegetables than to the works of human art, it is more probable that its cause resembles the cause of the former than that of the latter, and its origin ought rather to be abscribed to generation or vegetation than to reason or design. Your conclusion, even according to your own principles, is therefore lame and defective.

Demea: Pray open up this argument a little farther, said *Demea*, for I do not rightly apprehend it in that concise manner in which you have expressed it.

Philo: Our friend *Cleanthes*, replied *Philo*, as you have heard, asserts that since no question of fact can be proved otherwise than by experience, the existence of a Deity admits not of proof from any other medium. The world, says he, resembles the works of human contrivance; therefore its cause must also resemble that of the other. Here we may remark that the operation of one very small part of nature, to wit, man, upon another very small part, to wit, that inanimate matter lying within his reach, is the rule by which *Cleanthes* judges of the origin of the whole; and he measures objects, so widely disproportioned, by the same individual standard. But to waive all objections drawn from this topic, I affirm that there are other parts of the universe (besides the machines of human invention) which bear still a greater resemblance to the fabric of the world, and which, therefore, afford a better conjecture concerning the universal origin of this system. These parts are animals and vegetables. The world plainly resembles more an animal or a vegetable than it does a watch or a knitting-loom. Its cause, therefore, it is more probable, resembles the cause of the former. The cause of the former is generation or vegetation. The cause, therefore, of the world we may infer to be something similar or analogous to generation or vegetation.

Demea: But how is it conceivable, said *Demea*, that the world can arise from anything similar to vegetation or generation?

Philo: Very easily, replied *Philo*. In like manner as a tree sheds its seed into the neighboring fields and produces other trees; so the great vegetable, the world, or this planetary system, produces within itself certain seeds which, being scattered into the surrounding chaos, vegetate into new worlds. A comet, for instance, is the seed of a world; and after it has been fully ripened, by passing from sun to sun, and star to star, it is at last tossed into the unformed elements which everywhere surround this universe, and immediately sprouts up into a new system.

Or if, for the sake of variety (for I see no other advantage) we should suppose this world to be an animal; a comet is the egg of this animal; and in like manner as an ostrich lays its egg in the sand, which, without any further care, hatches the egg and produces a new animal, so. . . .

Demea: I understand you, says *Demea:* But what wild, arbitrary suppositions are these? What *data* have you for such extraordinary conclusions? And is the slight, imaginary resemblance of the world to a vegetable or an animal sufficient to establish the same inference with regard to both? Objects which are in general so widely different; ought they to be a standard for each other?

Philo: Right, cries *Philo:* This is the topic on which I have all along insisted. I have still asserted that we have no *data* to establish any system of cosmogony. Our experience, so imperfect in itself and so limited both in extent and duration, can afford us no probable conjecture concerning the whole of things. But if we must needs fix on some hypothesis, by what rule, pray, ought we to determine our choice? Is there any other rule than the great similarity of the objects compared? And does not a plant or an animal, which springs from vegetation or generation, bear a stronger resemblance to the world than does any artificial machine, which arises from reason and design?

Demea: But what is this vegetation and generation of which you talk? said *Demea*. Can you explain their operations, and anatomize that fine internal structure on which they depend?

Philo: As much, at least, replied *Philo*, as *Cleanthes* can explain the operations of reason, or anatomize that internal structure on which *it* depends. But without any such elaborate disquisitions, when I see an animal, I infer that it sprang from generation; and that with as great certainty as you conclude a house to have been reared by design. These words *generation, reason* mark only certain powers and energies in nature whose effects are known, but whose essence is incomprehensible; and one of these principles, more than the other, has no privilege for being made a standard to the whole of nature.

In reality, *Demea*, it may reasonably be expected that the larger the views are which we take of things, the better will they conduct us in our conclusions concerning such extraordinary and such magnificent subjects. In this little corner of the world alone, there are four principles, *reason, instinct, generation, vegetation*, which are similar to each other, and are the causes of similar effects. What a number of other principles may we naturally suppose in the immense extent and variety of the universe could we travel from planet to planet, and from system to system, in order to examine each part of this mighty fabric? Any one of these four principles above mentioned (and a hundred others which lie open to our conjecture) may afford us a theory by which to judge of the origin of the world; and it is a palpable and egregious partiality to confine our view entirely to that principle by which our own minds operate. Were this principle more intelligible on that account, such a partiality might be somewhat excusable: But reason, in its internal fabric and structure, is really as little known to us as instinct or vegetation; and, perhaps even that vague, undeterminate word "nature" to which the vulgar refer everything is not at the bottom more inexplicable. The effects of these principles are all known to us from experience; but the principles themselves and their manner of operation are totally unknown: Nor is it less intelligible or less conformable to experience to say that the world arose by vegetation, from a seed shed by another world, than to say that it arose from a divine reason or contrivance, according to the sense in which *Cleanthes* understands it.

Demea: But methinks, said *Demea*, if the world had a vegetative quality and could sow the seeds of new worlds into the infinite chaos, this power would be still an additional argument for design in its author. For whence could arise so wonderful a faculty but from design? Or how can order spring from anything which perceives not that order which it bestows?

Philo: You need only look around you, replied *Philo*, to satisfy yourself with regard to this question. A tree bestows order and organization on that tree which springs from it, without knowing the order: An animal in the same manner on its offspring: A bird on its nest; and instances of this kind are even more frequent in the world than those of order which arise from reason and contrivance. To say that all this order in animals and vegetables proceeds ultimately from design is begging the question; nor can that great point be ascertained otherwise than by proving, *a priori*, both that order is, from its nature, inseparably attached to thought, and that it can never of itself or from original unknown principles belong to matter.

But further, *Demea*, this objection which you urge can never be made use of by *Cleanthes*, without renouncing a defence which he has already made against one of my objections. When I inquired concerning the cause of that supreme reason and intelligence into which he resolves everything, he told me that the impossibility of satisfying such inquiries could never be admitted as an objection in any species of philosophy. *We must stop somewhere,* says he; *nor is it ever within the reach of human capacity to explain ultimate causes or show the last connections of any objects. It is sufficient if any steps, so far as we go, are supported by experience and observation.* Now, that vegetation and generation, as well as reason, are experienced to be principles of order in nature is undeniable. If I rest my system of cosmogony on the former, preferably to the latter, it is at my choice. The matter seems entirely arbitrary. And when *Cleanthes* asks me what is the cause of my great vegetative or generative faculty, I am equally entitled to ask him the cause of his great reasoning principle. These questions we have agreed to forbear on both sides; and it is chiefly his interest on the present occasion to stick to this agreement. Judging by our limited and imperfect experience, generation has some privileges above reason: For we see every day the latter arise from the former, never the former from the latter.

Compare, I beseech you, the consequences on both sides. The world, say I, resembles an animal; therefore it is an animal, therefore it arose from generation. The steps, I confess, are wide; yet there is some small appearance of analogy in each step. The world, says *Cleanthes*, resembles a machine; therefore it is a machine, therefore it arose from design. The steps are here equally wide, and the analogy less striking. And if he pretends to carry on *my* hypothesis a step further, and to infer design or reason from the great principle of generation on which I insist, I may, with better authority, use the same freedom to push further his hypothesis, and infer a divine generation or theogony from his principle of reason. I have at least some faint shadow of experience, which is the utmost that can ever be attained in the present subject. Reason, in innumerable instances, is observed to arise from the principle of generation, and never to arise from any other principle.

Hesiod and all the ancient mythologists were so struck with this analogy that they universally explained the origin of nature from an animal birth, and copulation. *Plato*, too, so far as he is intelligible, seems to have adopted some such notion in his *Timaeus*.

The *Brahmins* assert that the world arose from an infinite spider, who spun this whole complicated mass from his bowels, and annihilates afterwards the whole or any part of it, by absorbing it again and resolving it into his own essence. Here is a species of cosmogony which appears to us ridiculous because a spider is a little contemptible animal whose operations we are never likely to take for a model of the whole universe. But still here is a new species of analogy, even in our globe. And were there a planet wholly inhabited by spiders (which is very possible), this inference would there appear as natural and irrefragable as that which in our planet ascribes the origin of all things to design and intelligence, as explained by *Cleanthes*. Why an orderly system may not be spun from the belly as well as from the brain, it will be difficult for him to give a satisfactory reason.

Cleanthes: I must confess, *Philo*, replied *Cleanthes*, that, of all men living, the task which you have undertaken, of raising doubts and objections, suits you best and seems, in a manner, natural and unavoidable to you. So great is your fertility of invention that I am not ashamed to acknowledge myself unable, on a sudden, to solve regularly such out-of-the-way difficulties as you incessantly start upon me; though I clearly see, in general, their fallacy and error. And I question not, but you are yourself, at present, in the same case, and have not the solution so ready as the objection; while you must be sensible that common sense and reason are entirely against you, and that such whimsies as you have delivered may puzzle but never can convince us.

Part VIII

Philo: What you ascribe to the fertility of my invention, replied *Philo*, is entirely owing to the nature of the subject. In subjects adapted to the narrow compass of human reason there is commonly but one determination which carries probability or conviction with it; and to a man of sound judgment all other suppositions but that one appear entirely absurd and chimerical. But in such questions as the present, a hundred contradictory views may preserve a kind of imperfect analogy, and invention has here full scope to exert itself. Without any great effort of thought, I believe that I could, in an instant, propose other systems of cosmogony which would have some faint appearance of truth; though it is a thousand, a million to one if either yours or any one of mine be the true system.

For instance, what if I should revive the old *Epicurean* hypothesis? This is commonly, and I believe justly, esteemed the most absurd system that has yet been proposed; yet I know not whether, with a few alterations, it might not be brought to bear a faint appearance of probability. Instead of supposing matter infinite, as *Epicurus* did, let us suppose it finite. A finite number of particles is only susceptible of finite transpositions; and it must happen, in an eternal duration, that every possible order or position must be tried an infinite number of times. This world, therefore, with all its events, even the most minute, has before been produced and destroyed, and will again be produced and destroyed, without any bounds and limitations. No one who has a conception of the powers of infinite, in comparison of finite, will ever scruple this determination.

Demea: But this supposes, said *Demea*, that matter can acquire motion without any voluntary agent or first mover.

Philo: And where is the difficulty, replied *Philo*, of that supposition? Every event, before experience, is equally difficult and incomprehensible; and every event, after experience, is equally easy and intelligible. Motion, in many instances, from gravity, from elasticity, from electricity, begins in matter, without any known voluntary agent; and to suppose always, in these cases, an unknown voluntary agent is mere hypothesis; and hypothesis attended with no advantages. The beginning of motion in matter itself is as conceivable *a priori* as its communication from mind and intelligence.

Besides, why may not motion have been propagated by impulse through all eternity, and the same stock of it, or nearly the same, be still upheld in the universe? As much as is lost by the composition of motion, as much is gained by its resolution. And whatever the causes are, the fact is certain that matter is and always has been in continual agitation, as far as human experience or tradition reaches. There is not probably, at present, in the whole universe, one particle of matter at absolute rest.

And this very consideration, too, continued *Philo*, which we have stumbled on in the course of the argument suggests a new hypothesis of cosmogony that is not absolutely absurd and improbable. Is there a system, an order, an economy of things, by which matter can preserve that perpetual agitation which seems essential to it, and yet maintain a constancy in the forms which it produces? There certainly is such an economy, for this is actually the case with the present world. The continual motion of matter, therefore, in less than infinite transpositions, must produce this economy or order; and, by its very nature, that order, when once established, supports itself for many ages if not to eternity. But wherever matter is so poised, arranged, and adjusted, as to continue in perpetual motion, and yet preserve a constancy in the forms, its situation must, of necessity, have all the same appearance of art and contrivance which we observe at present. All the parts of each form must have a relation to each other and to the whole; and the whole itself must have a relation to the other parts of the universe, to the element in which the form subsists, to the materials with which it repairs its waste and decay, and to every other form which is hostile or friendly. A defect in any of these particulars destroys the form; and the matter of which it is composed is again set loose, and is thrown into irregular motions and fermentations till it unite itself to some other regular form. If no such form be prepared to receive it, and if there be a great quantity of this corrupted matter in the universe, the universe itself is entirely disordered, whether it be the feeble embryo of a world in its first beginnings that is thus destroyed, or the rotten carcass of one languishing in old age and infirmity. In either case, a chaos ensues till finite though innumerable revolutions produce, at last, some forms whose parts and organs are so adjusted as to support the forms amidst a continued succession of matter.

Suppose (for we shall endeavor to vary the expression) that matter were thrown into any position by a blind, unguided force; it is evident that this first position must, in all probability be the most confused and most disorderly imaginable, without any resemblance to those works of human contrivance which, along with a symmetry of parts, discover an adjustment of means to ends and a tendency to self-preservation. If the actuating force cease after this operation, matter must remain forever in disorder, and continue an immense chaos, without any proportion or activity. But suppose that the actuating force, whatever it be, still continues in matter, this first position will immediately give place to a second which will likewise, in all probability, be as disorderly as the first, and so on through many successions of changes and revolutions. No particular order or position ever continues a moment unaltered. The original force, still remaining in activity, gives a perpetual restlessness to matter. Every possible situation is produced, and instantly destroyed. If a glimpse or dawn of order appears for a moment, it is instantly hurried away and confounded by that never-ceasing force which actuates every part of matter.

Thus the universe goes on for many ages in a continued succession of chaos and disorder. But is it not possible that it may settle at last, so as not to lose its motion and active force (for that we have supposed inherent in it), yet so as to preserve a uniformity of appearance, amidst the continual motion and fluctuation of its parts? This we find to be the case with the universe at present. Every individual is perpetually changing, and every part of every individual; and yet the whole remains, in appearance, the same. May we not hope for such a position or rather be assured of it from the eternal revolutions of unguided matter; and may not this account for all the appearing wisdom and contrivance which is in the universe? Let us contemplate the subject a little, and we shall find that this adjustment if attained by matter of a seeming stability in the forms, with a real and perpetual revolution or motion of parts, affords a plausible, if not a true, solution of the difficulty.

It is in vain, therefore, to insist upon the uses of the parts in animals or vegetables, and their curious adjustment to each other. I would fain know how an animal could subsist unless its parts were so adjusted? Do we not find that it immediately perishes whenever this adjustment ceases, and that its matter, corrupting, tries some new form? It happens indeed that the parts of the world are so well adjusted that some regular form immediately lays claim to this corrupted matter; And if it were not so, could the world subsist? Must it not dissolve, as well as the animal, and pass through new positions and situations till in great but finite succession it fall, at last, into the present or some such order?

Cleanthes: It is well, replied *Cleanthes*, you told us that this hypothesis was suggested on a sudden, in the course of the argument. Had you had leisure to examine it, you would soon have perceived the insuperable objections to which it is exposed. No form, you say, can subsist unless it possess those powers and organs requisite for its subsistence; some new order or economy must be tried, and so on, without intermission, till at last some order which can support and maintain itself is fallen upon. But according to this hypothesis, whence arise the many conveniences and advantages which men and all animals possess? Two eyes, two ears are not absolutely necessary for the subsistence of the species. Human race might have been propagated and preserved without horses, dogs, cows, sheep, and those innumerable fruits and products which serve to our satisfaction and enjoyment. If no camels had been created for the use of man in the sandy deserts of Africa and Arabia, would the world have been dissolved? If no loadstone had been framed to give that wonderful and useful direction to the needle, would human society and the human kind have been immediately extinguished? Though the maxims of nature be in general very frugal, yet instances of this kind are far from being rare; and any one of them is a sufficient proof of design, and of a benevolent design, which gave rise to the order and arrangement of the universe.

Philo: At least, you may safely infer, said *Philo*, that the foregoing hypothesis is so far incomplete and imperfect, which I shall not scruple to allow. But can we ever reasonably expect greater success in any attempts of this nature? Or can we ever hope to erect a system of cosmogony that will be liable to no exceptions, and will contain no circumstance repugnant to our limited and imperfect experience of the analogy of nature? Your theory itself cannot surely pretend to any such advantage; even though you have run into *Anthropomorphism*, the better to preserve a conformity to common experience. Let us once more put it to trial. In all instances which we have ever seen, ideas are copied from real objects, and are ectypal, not archetypal, to express myself in learned terms. You reverse this order and give thought the precedence. In all instances which we have ever seen, thought has no influence upon matter except where that matter is so conjoined with it as to have an equal reciprocal influence upon it. No animal can move immediately anything but the members of its own body; and, indeed, the equality of action and reaction seems to be an universal law of nature: But your theory implies a contradiction to this experience. These instances, with many more which it were easy to collect (particularly the supposition of a mind or system of thought that is eternal or, in other words, an animal ingenerable and immortal) these instances, I say, may teach all of us sobriety in condemning each other, and let us see that as no system of this kind ought ever to be received from a slight analogy, so neither ought any to be rejected on account of a small incongruity. For that is an inconvenience from which we can justly pronounce no one to be exempted.

All religious systems, it is confessed, are subject to great and insuperable difficulties. Each disputant triumphs in his turn, while he carries on an offensive war, and exposes the absurdities, barbarities, and pernicious tenets of his antagonist. But all of them, on the whole, prepare a complete triumph for the skeptic, who tells them that no system ought ever to be embraced with regard to such subjects: For this plain reason, that no absurdity ought ever to be assented to with regard to any subject. A total suspense of judgment is here our only reasonable resource. And if every attack, as is commonly observed, and no defence among theologians is successful, how complete must be *his* victory who remains always, with all mankind, on the offensive, and has himself no fixed station or abiding city which he is ever, on any occasion, obliged to defend?

Part IX

Demea: But if so many difficulties attend the argument *a posteriori*, said *Demea*, had we not better adhere to that simple and sublime argument *a priori* which, by offering to us infallible demonstration, cuts off at once all doubt and difficulty? By this argument, too, we may prove the *Infinity* of the Divine Attributes, which, I am afraid, can never be ascertained with certainty from any other topic. For how can an effect which either is finite or, for aught we know, may be so; how can such an effect, I say, prove an infinite cause? The unity, too, of the Divine Nature it is very difficult, if not absolutely impossible, to deduce merely from contemplating the works of Nature; nor will the uniformity alone of the plan, even were it allowed, give us any assurance of that attribute. Whereas the argument *a priori*. . .

Cleanthes: You seem to reason, *Demea*, interposed *Cleanthes*, as if those advantages and conveniences in the abstract argument were full proofs of its solidity. But it is first proper, in my opinion, to determine what argument of this nature you choose to insist on; and we shall afterwards, from itself, better than from its *useful* consequences, endeavor to determine what value we ought to put upon it.

Demea: The argument, replied *Demea*, which I would insist on is the common one. Whatever exists must have a cause or reason of its existence, it being absolutely impossible for anything to produce itself or be the cause of its own existence. In mounting up, therefore, from effects to causes, we must either go on in tracing an infinite succession, without any ultimate cause at all, or must at last have recourse to some ultimate cause that is *necessarily* existent: Now, that the first supposition is absurd may be thus proved. In the infinite chain or succession of causes and effects, each single effect is determined to exist by the power and efficacy of that cause which immediately preceded; but the whole eternal chain or succession, taken together, is not determined or caused by anything: And yet it is evident that it requires a cause or reason, as much as any particular object which begins to exist in time. The question is still reasonable why this particular succession of causes existed from eternity, and not any other succession or no succession at all. If there be no necessarily existent being, any supposition which can be formed is equally possible; nor is there any more absurdity in nothing's having existed from eternity than there is in that succession of causes which constitutes the universe. What was it, then, which determined something to exist rather than nothing, and bestowed being on a particular possibility, exclusive of the rest? *External causes*, there are supposed to be none. *Chance* is a word without a meaning. Was it *nothing*? But that can never produce anything. We must, therefore, have recourse to a necessarily existent Being who carries the *reason* of his existence in himself; and who cannot be supposed not to exist, without an express contradiction. There is, consequently, such a Being—that is, there is a Deity.

Cleanthes: I shall not leave it to *Philo*, said *Cleanthes* (though I know that the starting objections is his chief delight), to point out the weakness of this metaphysical reasoning. It seems to me so obviously ill-grounded, and at the same time of so little consequence to the cause of true piety and religion, that I shall myself venture to show the fallacy of it.

I shall begin with observing that there is an evident absurdity in pretending to demonstrate a matter of fact, or to prove it by any arguments *a priori*. Nothing is demonstrable unless the contrary implies a contradiction. Nothing that is distinctly conceivable implies a contradiction. Whatever we conceive as existent, we can also conceive as non-existent. There is no being, therefore, whose non-existence implies a contradiction. Consequently there is no being whose existence is demonstrable. I propose this argument as entirely decisive, and am willing to rest the whole controversy upon it.

It is pretended that the Deity is a necessarily existent being; and this necessity of his existence is attempted to be explained by asserting that, if we knew his whole essence or nature, we should perceive it to be as impossible for him not to exist, as for twice two not to be four. But it is evident that this can never happen, while our faculties remain the same as at present. It will still be possible for us, at any time, to conceive the non-existence of what we formerly conceived to exist; nor can the mind ever lie under a necessity of supposing any object to remain always in being; in the same manner as we lie under a necessity of always conceiving twice two to be four. The words, therefore, "necessary existence" have no meaning; or, which is the same thing, none that is consistent.

But further, why may not the material universe be the necessarily existent Being, according to this pretended explication of necessity? We dare not affirm that we know all the qualities of matter; and, for aught we can determine, it may contain some qualities which, were they known, would make its non-existence appear as great a contradiction as that twice two is five. I find only one argument employed to prove that the material world is not the necessarily existent Being; and this argument is derived from the contingency both of the matter and the form of the world. "Any particle of matter," it is said, "may be *conceived* to be annihilated; and any form may be *conceived* to be altered. Such an annihilation or alteration, therefore, is not impossible"[18] But it seems a great partiality not to perceive that the same argument extends equally to the Deity, so far as we have any conception of him; and that the mind can at least imagine him to be non-existent, or his attributes to be altered. It must be some unknown, inconceivable qualities which can make his non-existence appear impossible or his attributes unalterable: And no reason can be assigned why these qualities may not belong to matter. As they are altogether unknown and inconceivable, they can never be proved incompatible with it.

Add to this that in tracing an eternal succession of objects it seems absurd to inquire for a general cause or first author. How can anything that exists from eternity have a cause, since that relation implies a priority in time and a beginning of existence?

In such a chain, too, or succession of objects, each part is caused by that which preceded it, and causes that which succeeds it. Where then is the difficulty? But the *whole*, you say, wants a cause. I answer that the uniting of these parts into a whole, like the uniting of several distinct countries into one kingdom, or several distinct members into one body, is performed merely by an arbitrary act of the mind, and has no influence on the nature of things. Did I show you the particular causes of each individual in a collection of twenty particles of matter, I should think it very unreasonable should you afterwards ask me what was the cause of the whole twenty. This is sufficiently explained in explaining the cause of the parts.

Philo: Though the reasonings which you have urged, *Cleanthes*, may well excuse me, said *Philo*, from starting any further difficulties; yet I cannot forbear insisting still upon another topic. It is

---

18. Dr. Clarke. [Samuel Clarke, 1675–1729, leading English theologian and philosopher, a follower of Sir Isaac Newton.]

observed by arithmeticians that the products of 9 compose always either 9 or some lesser product of 9 if you add together all the characters of which any of the former products is composed. Thus, of 18, 27, 36, which are products of 9, you make 9 by adding 1 to 8, 2 to 7, 3 to 6. Thus 369 is a product also of 9; and if you add 3, 6, and 9, you make 18, a lesser product of 9.[19] To a superficial observer so wonderful a regularity may be admired as the effect either of chance or design; but a skilful algebraist immediately concludes it to be the work of necessity, and demonstrates that it must forever result from the nature of these numbers. Is it not probable, I ask, that the whole economy of the universe is conducted by a like necessity, though no human algebra can furnish a key which solves the difficulty? And instead of admiring the order of natural beings, may it not happen that, could we penetrate into the intimate nature of bodies, we should clearly see why it was absolutely impossible they could ever admit of any other disposition? So dangerous is it to introduce this idea of necessity into the present question! And so naturally does it afford an inference directly opposite to the religious hypothesis!

But dropping all these abstractions, continued *Philo*, and confining ourselves to more familiar topics, I shall venture to add an observation that the argument *a priori* has seldom been found very convincing, except to people of a metaphysical head who have accustomed themselves to abstract reasoning, and who, finding from mathematics that the understanding frequently leads to truth through obscurity, and contrary to first appearances, have transferred the same habit of thinking to subjects where it ought not to have place. Other people, even of good sense and the best inclined to religion, feel always some deficiency in such arguments, though they are not perhaps able to explain distinctly where it lies, a certain proof that men ever did and ever will derive their religion from other sources than from this species of reasoning.

19. *Republique des Lettres,* Aug. 1685. [The article referred to is by Fontenelle, and it appeared in Pierre Bayle's *Nouvelles de la Republique des Lettres*, Sept. 1685, art. II.]

Part X

Demea: It is my opinion, I own, replied *Demea*, that each man feels, in a manner, the truth of religion within his own breast; and, from a consciousness of his imbecility and misery rather than from any reasoning, is led to seek protection from that Being on whom he and all nature are dependent. So anxious or so tedious are even the best scenes of life that futurity is still the object of all our hopes and fears. We incessantly look forward and endeavor, by prayers, adoration, and sacrifice, to appease those unknown powers whom we find, by experience, so able to afflict and oppress us. Wretched creatures that we are! What resource for us amidst the innumerable ills of life did not religion suggest some methods of atonement, and appease those terrors with which we are incessantly agitated and tormented?

Philo: I am indeed persuaded, said *Philo*, that the best and indeed the only method of bringing everyone to a due sense of religion is by just representations of the misery and wickedness of men. And for that purpose a talent of eloquence and strong imagery is more requisite than that of reasoning and argument. For is it necessary to prove what everyone feels within himself? It is only necessary to make us feel it, if possible, more intimately and sensibly.

Demea: The people, indeed, replied *Demea*, are sufficiently convinced of this great and melancholy truth. The miseries of life, the unhappiness of man, the general corruptions of our nature, the unsatisfactory enjoyment of pleasures, riches, honors; these phrases have become almost proverbial in all languages. And who can doubt of what all men declare from their own immediate feeling and experience?

Philo: In this point, said *Philo*, the learned are perfectly agreed with the vulgar; and in all letters, *sacred* and *profane*, the topic of human misery has been insisted on with the most pathetic eloquence that sorrow and melancholy could inspire. The poets, who speak from sentiment, without a system, and whose testimony has therefore the more authority, abound in images of this nature. From *Homer* down to *Dr. Young*,[20] the whole inspired tribe have ever been sensible that no other representation of things would suit the feeling and observation of each individual.

Demea: As to authorities, replied *Demea*, you need not seek them. Look round this library of *Cleanthes*. I shall venture to affirm that, except authors of particular sciences, such as chemistry or botany, who have no occasion to treat of human life, there is scarce one of those innumerable writers from whom the sense of human misery has not, in some passage or other, extorted a complaint and confession of it. At least, the chance is entirely on that side; and no one author has ever, so far as I can recollect, been so extravagant as to deny it.

Philo: There you must excuse me, said *Philo: Leibniz* has denied it, and is perhaps the first[21] who ventured upon so bold and paradoxical an opinion; at least, the first who made it essential to his philosophical system.

Demea: And by being the first, replied *Demea*, might he not have been sensible of his error? For is this a subject in which philosophers can propose to make discoveries especially in so late an age? And can any man hope by a simple denial (for the subject scarcely admits of reasoning) to bear down the united testimony of mankind, founded on sense and consciousness?

And why should man, added he, pretend to an exemption from the lot of all other animals? The whole earth, believe me, *Philo*, is cursed and polluted. A perpetual war is kindled amongst all living creatures. Necessity, hunger, want stimulate the strong and courageous: fear, anxiety, terror agitate the weak and infirm. The first entrance into life gives anguish to the new-born infant and to its wretched parent: weakness, impotence, distress attend each stage of that life, and it is, at last, finished in agony and horror.

Philo: Observe, too, says *Philo*, the curious artifices of nature in order to embitter the life of every living being. The stronger prey upon the weaker and keep them in perpetual terror and anxiety. The weaker, too, in their turn, often prey upon the stronger, and

20. [Hume was apparently referring to the prolific poet, Edward Young, 1683–1765.]

21. That sentiment had been maintained by *Dr. King* and some few others before Leibniz, though by none of so great fame as that German philosopher. [Dr. William King, 1650–1729, was the archbishop of Dublin. He wrote *De Origine Mali*, The Origins of Evil, published in 1702.]

vex and molest them without relaxation. Consider that innumerable race of insects, which either are bred on the body of each animal or, flying about, infix their stings in him. These insects have others still less than themselves which torment them. And thus on each hand, before and behind, above and below, every animal is surrounded with enemies which incessantly seek his misery and destruction.

Demea: Man alone, said *Demea*, seems to be, in part, an exception to this rule. For by combination in society he can easily master lions, tigers, and bears, whose greater strength and agility naturally enable them to prey upon him.

Philo: On the contrary, it is here chiefly, cried *Philo*, that the uniform and equal maxims of nature are most apparent. Man, it is true, can, by combination, surmount all his *real* enemies and become master of the whole animal creation: But does he not immediately raise up to himself *imaginary* enemies, the demons of his fancy, who haunt him with superstitious terrors and blast every enjoyment of life? His pleasure, as he imagines, becomes in their eyes a crime: His food and repose give them umbrage and offence; his very sleep and dreams furnish new materials to anxious fear: And even death, his refuge from every other ill, presents only the dread of endless and innumerable woes. Nor does the wolf molest more the timid flock than superstition does the anxious breast of wretched mortals.

Besides, consider, *Demea:* This very society by which we surmount those wild beasts, our natural enemies, what new enemies does it not raise to us? What woe and misery does it not occasion? Man is the greatest enemy of man. Oppression, injustice, contempt, contumely, violence, sedition, war, calumny, treachery, fraud; by these they mutually torment each other, and they would soon dissolve that society which they had formed were it not for the dread of still greater ills which must attend their separation.

Demea: But though these external insults, said *Demea*, from animals, from men, from all the elements, which assault us form a frightful catalogue of woes, they are nothing in comparison of those which arise within ourselves, from the distempered condition of our mind and body. How many lie under the lingering torment of diseases? Hear the pathetic enumeration of the great poet.

> Intestine stone and ulcer, colic-pangs,
> Demoniac frenzy, moping melancholy,
> And moon-struck madness, pining atrophy,
> Marasmus, and wide-wasting pestilence.

Dire was the tossing, deep the groans: *Despair*
Tended the sick, busiest from couch to couch.
And over them triumphant *Death* his dart
Shook: but delay'd to strike, though oft invok'd
With vows, as their chief good and final hope.[22]

The disorders of the mind, continued *Demea*, though more secret, are not perhaps less dismal and vexatious. Remorse, shame, anguish, rage, disappointment, anxiety, fear, dejection, despair: who has ever passed through life without cruel inroads from these tormentors? How many have scarcely ever felt any better sensations? Labor and poverty, so abhorred by everyone, are the certain lot of the far greater number: And those few privileged persons who enjoy ease and opulence never reach contentment or true felicity. All the goods of life united would not make a very happy man: But all the ills united would make a wretch indeed; and any one of them almost (and who can be free from every one), nay, often the absence of one good (and who can possess all) is sufficient to render life ineligible.

Were a stranger to drop on a sudden into this world, I would show him, as a specimen of its ills, a hospital full of diseases, a prison crowded with malefactors and debtors, a field of battle strewed with carcases, a fleet foundering in the ocean, a nation languishing under tyranny, famine, or pestilence. To turn the gay side of life to him and give him a notion of its pleasures; whither should I conduct him? to a ball, to an opera, to court? He might justly think that I was only showing him a diversity of distress and sorrow.

Philo: There is no evading such striking instances, said *Philo*, but by apologies which still further aggravate the charge. Why have all men, I ask, in all ages, complained incessantly of the miseries of life? . . . They have no just reason, says one: These complaints proceed only from their discontented, repining, anxious disposition. . . . And can there possibly, I reply, be a more certain foundation of misery than such a wretched temper?

But if they were really as unhappy as they pretend, says my antagonist, why do they remain in life? . . .

Not satisfied with life, afraid of death.

22. [Milton: *Paradise Lost*, Bk. XI.]

This is the secret chain, say I, that holds us. We are terrified, not bribed to the continuance of our existence.

It is only a false delicacy, he may insist, which a few refined spirits indulge, and which has spread these complaints among the whole race of mankind. . . . And what is this delicacy, I ask, which you blame? Is it anything but a greater sensibility to all the pleasures and pains of life? And if the man of a delicate, refined temper, by being so much more alive than the rest of the world, is only so much more unhappy, what judgment must we form in general of human life?

Let men remain at rest, says our adversary, and they will be easy. They are willing artificers of their own misery. . . . No! reply I: An anxious languor follows their repose; disappointment, vexation, trouble, their activity and ambition.

Cleanthes: I can observe something like what you mention in some others, replied *Cleanthes;* but I confess I feel little or nothing of it in myself, and hope that it is not so common as you represent it.

Demea: If you feel not human misery yourself, cried *Demea,* I congratulate you on so happy a singularity. Others, seemingly the most prosperous, have not been ashamed to vent their complaints in the most melancholy strains. Let us attend to the great, the fortunate emperor, *Charles V,*[23] when, tired with human grandeur, he resigned all his extensive dominions into the hands of his son. In the last harangue which he made on that memorable occasion, he publicly avowed *that the greatest prosperities which he had ever enjoyed had been mixed with so many adversities that he might truly say he had never enjoyed any satisfaction or contentment.* But did the retired life in which he sought for shelter afford him any greater happiness? If we may credit his son's account, his repentance commenced the very day of his resignation.

Cicero's fortune, from small beginnings, rose to the greatest luster and renown; yet what pathetic complaints of the ills of life do his familiar letters, as well as philosophical discourses, contain? And suitably to his own experience, he introduces *Cato,* the great, the fortunate *Cato* protesting in his old age that had he a new life in his offer he would reject the present.

Ask yourself, ask any of your acquaintance, whether they would live over again the last ten or twenty years of their life. No! but the next twenty, they say, will be better:

23. [Charles V, 1500–1558, was king of Spain and Holy Roman Emperor. He retired from his thrones in 1556 and 1558.]

> And from the dregs of life, hope to receive
> What the first sprightly running could not give.[24]

Thus, at last, they find (such is the greatness of human misery, it reconciles even contradictions) that they complain at once of the shortness of life and of its vanity and sorrow.

Philo: And is it possible, *Cleanthes*, said *Philo*, that after all these reflections, and infinitely more which might be suggested, you can still persevere in your anthropomorphism, and assert the moral attributes of the Deity, his justice, benevolence, mercy, and rectitude, to be of the same nature with these virtues in human creatures? His power, we allow, is infinite; whatever he wills is executed: But neither man nor any other animal is happy; therefore, he does not will their happiness. His wisdom is infinite; He is never mistaken in choosing the means to any end; But the course of nature tends not to human or animal felicity: Therefore, it is not established for that purpose. Through the whole compass of human knowledge there are no inferences more certain and infallible than these. In what respect, then, do his benevolence and mercy resemble the benevolence and mercy of men?

Epicurus' old questions are yet unanswered.

Is he willing to prevent evil, but not able? then is he impotent. Is he able, but not willing? then is he malevolent. Is he both able and willing? whence then is evil?

You ascribe, *Cleanthes* (and I believe justly), a purpose and intention to nature. But what, I beseech you, is the object of that curious artifice and machinery which she had displayed in all animals? The preservation alone of individuals, and propagation of the species? It seems enough for her purpose, if such a rank be barely upheld in the universe, without any care or concern for the happiness of the members that compose it. No resource for this purpose: No machinery in order merely to give pleasure or ease: No fund of pure joy and contentment: No indulgence without some want or necessity accompanying it. At least, the few phenomena of this nature are overbalanced by opposite phenomena of still greater importance.

Our sense of music, harmony, and indeed beauty of all kinds, gives satisfaction, without being absolutely necessary to the preservation and propagation of the species. But what racking pains, on the other hand, arise from gouts, gravels, megrims, toothaches, rheumatisms, where the injury to the animal machinery is either small or incurable? Mirth, laughter, play, frolic seem gratuitous

24. [John Dryden, *Aureng-Zebe*, Act IV, sc. 1.]

satisfactions which have no further tendency; spleen, melancholy, discontent, superstition are pains of the same nature. How then does the divine benevolence display itself, in the sense of you anthropormorphites? None but we mystics, as you were pleased to call us, can account for this strange mixture of phenomena, by deriving it from attributes infinitely perfect but incomprehensible.

Cleanthes: And have you, at last, said *Cleanthes* smiling, betrayed your intentions, *Philo?* Your long agreement with *Demea* did indeed a little surprise me, but I find you were all the while erecting a concealed battery against me. And I must confess that you have now fallen upon a subject worthy of your noble spirit of opposition and controversy. If you can make out the present point, and prove mankind to be unhappy or corrupted, there is an end at once of all religion. For to what purpose establish the natural attributes of the Deity, while the moral are still doubtful and uncertain?

Demea: You take umbrage very easily, replied *Demea*, at opinions the most innocent and the most generally received, even amongst the religious and devout themselves; and nothing can be more surprising than to find a topic like this—concerning the wickedness and misery of man—charged with no less than atheism and profaneness. Have not all pious divines and preachers who have indulged their rhetoric on so fertile a subject; have they not easily, I say, given a solution of any difficulties which may attend it? This world is but a point in comparison of the universe; this life but a moment in comparison of eternity. The present evil phenomena, therefore, are rectified in other regions, and in some future period of existence. And the eyes of men, being then opened to larger views of things, see the whole connection of general laws, and trace, with adoration, the benevolence and rectitude of the Diety through all the mazes and intricacies of his providence.

Cleanthes: No! replied *Cleanthes*, no! These arbitrary suppositions can never be admitted, contrary to matter of fact, visible and uncontroverted. Whence can any cause be known but from its known effects? Whence can any hypothesis be proved but from the apparent phenomena? To establish one hypothesis upon another is building entirely in the air; and the utmost we ever attain by these conjectures and fictions is to ascertain the bare possibility of our opinion, but never can we, upon such terms, establish its reality.

The only method of supporting divine benevolence (and it is what I willingly embrace) is to deny absolutely the misery and wickedness of man. Your representations are exaggerated; your melancholy views mostly fictitious; your inferences contrary to fact and experience. Health is more common than sickness: Pleasure than pain: Happiness than misery. And for one vexation which we meet with, we attain, upon computation, a hundred enjoyments.

Philo: Admitting your position, replied *Philo*, which yet is extremely doubtful, you must at the same time allow that, if pain be less frequent than pleasure, it is infinitely more violent and durable. One hour of it is often able to outweigh a day, a week, a month of our common insipid enjoyments; and how many days, weeks, and months are passed by several in the most acute torments? Pleasure, scarcely in one instance, is ever able to reach ecstasy and rapture: And in no one instance can it continue for any time at its highest pitch and altitude. The spirits evaporate, the nerves relax, the fabric is disordered, and the enjoyment quickly degenerates into fatigue and uneasiness. But pain often, good God, how often! rises to torture and agony; and the longer it continues, it becomes still more genuine agony and torture. Patience is exhausted, courage languishes, melancholy seizes us, and nothing terminates our misery but the removal of its cause or another event which is the sole cure of all evil, but which, from our natural folly, we regard with still greater horror and consternation.

But not to insist upon these topics, continued *Philo*, though most obvious, certain, and important, I must use the freedom to admonish you, *Cleanthes*, that you have put the controversy upon a most dangerous issue, and are unawares introducing a total skepticism into the most essential articles of natural and revealed theology. What! no method of fixing a just foundation for religion unless we allow the happiness of human life, and maintain a continued existence even in this world, with all our present pains, infirmities, vexations, and follies, to be eligible and desirable! But this is contrary to everyone's feeling and experience; it is contrary to an authority so established as nothing can subvert. No decisive proofs can ever be produced against this authority; nor is it possible for you to compute, estimate, and compare all the pains and all the pleasures in the lives of all men and of all animals: And thus, by your resting the whole system of religion on a point which, from its very nature, must forever be uncertain, you tacitly confess that that system is equally uncertain.

But allowing you what never will be believed, at least, what you never possibly can prove, that animal or, at least, human happiness in this life exceeds its misery, you have yet done nothing; for this is not, by any means, what we expect from infinite power, infinite wisdom, and infinite goodness. Why is there any misery at all in the world? Not by chance, surely. From some cause then. Is it from the intention of the Deity? But he is perfectly benevolent. Is it contrary to his intention? But he is almighty. Nothing can shake the solidity of this reasoning, so short, so clear, so decisive, except we assert that these subjects exceed all human capacity, and that our common measures of truth and falsehood are not applicable to them; a topic which I have all along insisted on, but which you have, from the beginning, rejected with scorn and indignation.

But I will be contented to retire still from this retrenchment, for I deny that you can ever force me in it. I will allow that pain or misery in man is *compatible* with infinite power and goodness in the Deity, even in your sense of these attributes: what are you advanced by all these concessions? A mere possible compatibility is not sufficient. You must *prove* these pure, unmixed and uncontrollable attributes from the present mixed and confused phenomena, and from these alone. A hopeful undertaking! Were the phenomena ever so pure and unmixed, yet, being finite, they would be insufficient for that purpose. How much more, where they are also so jarring and discordant!

Here, *Cleanthes*, I find myself at ease in my argument. Here I triumph. Formerly, when we argued concerning the natural attributes of intelligence and design, I needed all my skeptical and metaphysical subtilty to elude your grasp. In many views of the universe and of its parts, particularly the latter, the beauty and fitness of final causes strike us with such irresistible force that all objections appear (what I believe they really are) mere cavils and sophisms; nor can we then imagine how it was ever possible for us to repose any weight on them. But there is no view of human life or of the condition of mankind from which, without the greatest violence, we can infer the moral attributes or learn that infinite benevolence, conjoined with infinite power and infinite wisdom, which we must discover by the eyes of faith alone. It is your turn now to tug the laboring oar, and to support your philosophical subtilties against the dictates of plain reason and experience.

Part XI

Cleanthes: I scruple not to allow, said *Cleanthes*, that I have been apt to suspect the frequent repetition of the word "infinite," which we meet with in all theological writers, to savor more of panegyric than of philosophy, and that any purposes of reasoning, and even of religion, would be better served were we to rest contented with more accurate and more moderate expressions. The terms "admirable," "excellent," "superlatively great," "wise," and "holy"; these sufficiently fill the imaginations of men, and anything beyond, besides that it leads into absurdities, has no influence on the affections or sentiments. Thus, in the present subject, if we abandon all human analogy, as seems your intention, *Demea*, I am afraid we abandon all religion and retain no conception of the great object of our adoration. If we preserve human analogy, we must forever find it impossible to reconcile any mixture of evil in the universe with infinite attributes; much less can we ever prove the latter from the former. But supposing the Author of Nature to be finitely perfect, though far exceeding mankind, a satisfactory account may then be given of natural and moral evil, and every untoward phenomenon be explained and adjusted. A lesser evil may then be chosen in order to avoid a greater; inconveniences be submitted to in order to reach a desirable end; and, in a word, benevolence, regulated by wisdom and limited by necessity, may produce just such a world as the present. You, *Philo*, who are so prompt at starting views and reflections and analogies, I would gladly hear, at length, without interruption, your opinion of this new theory; and if it deserve our attention, we may afterwards, at more leisure, reduce it into form.

Philo: My sentiments, replied *Philo*, are not worth being made a mystery of; and, therefore, without any ceremony, I shall deliver what occurs to me with regard to the present subject. It must, I think, be allowed that, if a very limited intelligence whom we shall suppose utterly unacquainted with the universe were assured that it were the production of a very good, wise, and powerful being, however finite, he would, from his conjectures, form *beforehand* a different notion of it from what we find it to be by experience; nor would he ever imagine, merely from these attributes of the cause of which he is informed, that the effect could be so full of vice and misery and disorder, as it appears in this life. Supposing now that this person were brought into the world, still assured that it was the workmanship of such a sublime and benevolent being, he might, perhaps, be surprised at the disappointment, but would never retract his former belief if founded on any very solid argument; since such a limited intelligence must be sensible of his own blindness and ignorance, and must allow that there may be many solutions of those phenomena which will forever escape his comprehension. But supposing, which is the real case with regard to man, that this creature is not antecedently convinced of a supreme intelligence, benevolent, and powerful, but is left to gather such a belief from the appearances of things; this entirely alters the case, nor will he ever find any reason for such a conclusion. He may be fully convinced of the narrow limits of his understanding, but this will not help him in forming an inference concerning the goodness of superior powers, since he must form that inference from what he knows, not from what he is ignorant of. The more you exaggerate his weakness and ignorance, the more diffident you render him, and give him the greater suspicion that such subjects are beyond the reach of his faculties. You are obliged, therefore, to reason with him merely from the known phenomena, and to drop every arbitrary supposition or conjecture.

Did I show you a house or palace where there was not one apartment convenient or agreeable; where the windows, doors, fires, passages, stairs, and the whole economy of the building were the source of noise, confusion, fatigue, darkness, and the extremes of heat and cold, you would certainly blame the contrivance, without any further examination. The architect would in vain display his subtilty, and prove to you that, if this door or that window were altered, greater ills would ensue. What he says may be strictly true: The alteration of one particular, while the other parts of the building remain, may only augment the inconveniences. But still you would assert in general that, if the architect had had skill and good intentions, he might have formed such a plan of the whole, and might have adjusted the parts in such a manner as would have remedied all or most of these inconveniences. His ignorance, or even your own ignorance of such a plan, will never convince you of the impossibility of it. If you find any inconveniences and deformities in the building, you will always, without enterting into any detail, condemn the architect.

In short, I repeat the question: Is the world, considered in general and as it appears to us in this life, different from what a man or such a limited being would, *beforehand*, expect from a very powerful, wise, and benevolent Deity? It must be strange prejudice to assert the contrary. And from thence I conclude that, however consistent the world may be, allowing certain suppositions and conjectures with the idea of such a Deity, it can never afford us an inference concerning his existence. The consistency is not absolutely denied, only the inference. Conjectures, especially where infinity is excluded from the divine attributes, may perhaps be sufficient to prove a consistency, but can never be foundations for any inference.

There seem to be *four* circumstances on which depend all or the greatest part of the ills that molest sensible creatures; and it is not impossible but all these circumstances may be necessary and unavoidable. We know so little beyond common life, or even of common life, that, with regard to the economy of a universe, there is no conjecture, however wild, which may not be just; nor any one, however plausible, which may not be erroneous. All that belongs to human understanding, in this deep ignorance and obscurity, is to be skeptical or at least cautious, and not to admit of any hypothesis whatever, much less of any which is supported by no appearance of probability. Now this I assert to be the case with regard to all the causes of evil and the circumstances on which it depends. None of them appear to human reason in the least degree necessary or unavoidable, nor can we suppose them such, without the utmost license of imagination.

The *first* circumstance which introduces evil is that contrivance or economy of the animal creation by which pains, as well as pleasures, are employed to excite all creatures to action, and make them vigilant in the great work of self-preservation. Now pleasure alone, in its various degrees, seems to human understanding sufficient for this purpose. All animals might be constantly in a state of enjoyment; but when urged by any of the necessities of nature, such as thirst, hunger, weariness; instead of pain, they might feel a diminution of pleasure by which they might be prompted to seek that object which is necessary to their subsistence. Men pursue pleasure as eagerly as they avoid pain; at least, they might have been so constituted. It seems, therefore, plainly possible to carry on the business of life without any pain. Why then is any animal ever rendered susceptible of such a sensation? If animals can be free from it an hour, they might enjoy a perpetual exemption from it, and it required as particular a contrivance of their organs to produce that feeling as to endow them with sight, hearing, or any of the senses. Shall we conjecture that such a contrivance was necessary, without any appearance of reason? And shall we build on that conjecture as on the most certain truth?

But a capacity of pain would not alone produce pain were it not for the *second* circumstance, viz., the conducting of the world by general laws; and this seems nowise necessary to a very perfect being. It is true, if everything were conducted by particular volitions, the course of nature would be perpetually broken, and no man could employ his reason in the conduct of life. But might not other particular volitions remedy this inconvenience? In short, might not the Deity exterminate all ill, wherever it were to be found, and produce all good, without any preparation or long progress of causes and effects?

Besides, we must consider that, according to the present economy of the world, the course of nature, though supposed exactly regular, yet to us appears not so, and many events are uncertain, and many disappoint our expectations. Health and sickness, calm and tempest, with an infinite number of other accidents whose causes are unknown and variable, have a great influence both on the fortunes of particular persons and on the prosperity of public societies: And indeed all human life, in a manner, depends on such accidents. A being, therefore, who knows the secret springs of the universe might easily, by particular volitions, turn all these accidents to the good of mankind and render the whole world happy, without discovering himself in any operation. A fleet whose purposes were salutary to society might always meet with a fair wind: Good princes enjoy sound health and long life: Persons born to power and authority be framed with good tempers and virtuous dispositions. A few such events as these, regularly and wisely conducted, would change the face of the world; and yet would no more seem to disturb the course of nature or confound human conduct than the present economy of things, where the causes are secret and variable and compounded. Some small touches given to *Caligula's* brain in his infancy might have converted him into a *Trajan*. One wave, a little higher than the rest, by burying *Caesar* and his fortune in the bottom of the ocean, might have restored liberty to a considerable part of mankind. There may, for aught we know, be good reasons why Providence interposes not in this manner, but they are unknown to us; And, though the mere supposition that such reasons exist may be sufficient to *save* the conclusion concerning the divine attributes, yet surely it can never be sufficient to *establish* that conclusion.

If everything in the universe be conducted by general laws, and if animals be rendered susceptible of pain, it scarcely seems possible but some ill must arise in the various shocks of matter and the various concurrence and opposition of general laws; but this ill would be very rare were it not for the *third* circumstance which I proposed to mention, viz., the great frugality with which all powers and faculties are distributed to every particular being. So well adjusted are the organs and capacities of all animals, and so well fitted to their preservation, that, as far as history or tradition reaches, there appears not to be any single species which has yet been extinguished in the universe. Every animal has the requisite endowments, but these endowments are bestowed with so scrupulous an economy that any considerable diminution must entirely destroy the creature. Wherever one power is increased, there is a proportional abatement in the others. Animals which excel in swiftness are commonly defective in force. Those which possess both are either imperfect in some of their senses or are oppressed with the most craving wants. The human species, whose chief excellence is reason and sagacity, is of all others the most necessitous, and the most deficient in bodily advantages; without clothes, without arms, without food, without lodging, without any convenience of life, except what they owe to their own skill and industry. In short, nature seems to have formed an exact calculation of the necessities of her creatures; and, like a *rigid master*, has afforded them little more powers or endowments than what are strictly sufficient to supply those necessities. An *indulgent parent* would have bestowed a large stock in order to guard against accidents, and secure the happiness and welfare of the creature in the most unfortunate concurrence of circumstances. Every course of life would not have been so surrounded with precipices that the least departure from the true path, by mistake or necessity, must involve us in misery and ruin. Some reserve, some fund, would have been provided to ensure happiness, nor would the powers and the necessities have been adjusted with so rigid an economy. The Author of Nature is inconceivably powerful; his force is supposed great, if not altogether inexhaustible nor is there any reason, as far as we can judge, to make him observe this strict frugality in his dealings with his creatures. It would have been better, were his power extremely limited, to have created fewer animals, and to have endowed these with more faculties for their happiness and preservation. A builder is never esteemed prudent who undertakes a plan beyond what his stock will enable him to finish.

In order to cure most of the ills of human life, I require not that man should have the wings of the eagle, the swiftness of the stag, the force of the ox, the arms of the lion, the scales of the crocodile or rhinoceros; much less do I demand the sagacity of an angel or cherubim. I am contented to take an increase in one single power or faculty of his soul. Let him be endowed with a greater propensity to industry and labor, a more vigorous spring and activity of mind, a more constant bent to business and application. Let the whole species possess naturally an equal diligence with that which many individuals are able to attain by habit and reflection, and the most beneficial consequences, without any allay of ill, is the immediate and necessary result of this endowment. Almost all the moral as well as natural evils of human life arise from idleness; and were our species, by the original constitution of their frame, exempt from this vice or infirmity, the perfect cultivation of land, the improvement of arts and manufactures, the exact execution of every office and duty, immediately follow; and men at once may fully reach that state of society which is so imperfectly attained by the best regulated government. But as industry is a power, and the most valuable of any, nature seems determined, suitably to her usual maxims, to bestow it on men with a very sparing hand; and rather to punish him severely for his deficiency in it than to reward him for his attainments. She has so contrived his frame that nothing but the most violent necessity can oblige him to labor; and she employs all his other wants to overcome, at least in part, the want of diligence, and to endow him with some share of a faculty of which she has thought fit naturally to bereave him. Here our demands may be allowed very humble, and therefore the more reasonable. If we required the endowments of superior penetration and judgment, of a more delicate taste of beauty, of a nicer sensibility to benevolence and friendship, we might be told that we impiously pretend to break the order of Nature, that we want to exalt ourselves into a higher rank of being, that the presents which we require, not being suitable to our state and condition, would only be pernicious to us. But it is hard, I dare to repeat it, it is hard that, being placed in a world so full of wants and necessities, where almost every being and element is either our foe or refuses its assistance; we should also have our own temper to struggle with, and should be deprived of that faculty which can alone fence against these multiplied evils.

The *fourth* circumstance whence arises the misery and ill of the universe is the inaccurate workmanship of all the springs and principles of the great machine of nature. It must be acknowledged that there are few parts of the universe which seem not to serve some purpose, and whose removal would not produce a visible defect and disorder in the whole. The parts hang all together, nor can one be touched without affecting the rest, in a greater or less degree. But at the same time, it must be observed that none of these parts or principles, however useful, are so accurately adjusted as to keep precisely within those bounds in which their utility consists; but they are, all of them, apt, on every occasion, to run into the one extreme or the other. One would imagine that this grand production had not received the last hand of the maker; so little finished is every part, and so coarse are the strokes with which it is executed. Thus the winds are requisite to convey the vapors along the surface of the globe, and to assist men in navigation: But how often, rising up to tempests and hurricanes, do they become pernicious? Rains are necessary to nourish all the plants and animals of the earth: But how often are they defective? how often excessive? Heat is requisite to all life and vegetation, but is not always found in the due proportion. On the mixture and secretion of the humors and juices of the body depend the health and prosperity of the animal: But the parts perform not regularly their proper function. What more useful than all the passions of the mind, ambition, vanity, love, anger? But how often do they break their bounds and cause the greatest convulsions in society? There is nothing so advantageous in the universe but what frequently becomes pernicious, by its excess or defect; nor has nature guarded, with the requisite accuracy, against all disorder or confusion. The irregularity is never perhaps so great as to destroy any species, but is often sufficient to involve the individuals in ruin and misery.

On the concurrence, then, of these *four* circumstances does all or the greatest part of natural evil depend. Were all living creatures incapable of pain, or were the world administered by particular volitions, evil never could have found access into the universe: And were animals endowed with a large stock of powers and faculties, beyond what strict necessity requires, or were the several springs and principles of the universe so accurately framed as to preserve always the just temperament and medium, there must have been very little ill in comparison of what we feel at present. What then

shall we pronounce on this occasion? Shall we say that these circumstances are not necessary, and that they might easily have been
altered in the contrivance of the universe? This decision seems too
presumptuous for creatures so blind and ignorant. Let us be more
modest in our conclusions. Let us allow that, if the goodness of the
Deity (I mean a goodness like the human) could be established on
any tolerable reasons *a priori*, these phenomena, however untoward, would not be sufficient to subvert that principle, but might
easily, in some unknown manner, be reconcilable to it. But let us
still assert that, as this goodness is not antecedently established but
must be inferred from the phenomena, there can be no grounds for
such an inference while there are so many ills in the universe, and
while these ills might so easily have been remedied, as far as human
understanding can be allowed to judge on such a subject. I am skeptic enough to allow that the bad appearances, notwithstanding all
my reasonings, may be compatible with such attributes as you suppose; but surely they can never prove these attributes. Such a conclusion cannot result from skepticism, but must arise from the
phenomena, and from our confidence in the reasonings which we
deduce from these phenomena.

Look round this universe. What an immense profusion of beings,
animated and organized, sensible and active! You admire this prodigious variety and fecundity. But inspect a little more narrowly
these living existences, the only beings worth regarding. How
hostile and destructive to each other! How insufficient all of them
for their own happiness! How contemptible or odious to the spec-
tator! The whole presents nothing but the idea of a blind nature, im-
pregnated by a great vivifying principle, and pouring forth from her
lap, without discernment or parental care, her maimed and abortive
children!

Here the Manichaean system[25] occurs as a proper hypothesis to
solve the difficulty; and, no doubt, in some respects it is very
specious and has more probability than the common hypothesis, by
giving a plausible account of the strange mixture of good and ill
which appears in life. But if we consider, on the other hand, the
perfect uniformity and agreement of the parts of the universe, we
shall not discover in it any marks of the combat of a malevolent
with a benevolent being. There is indeed an opposition of pains and
pleasures in the feelings of sensible creatures; But are not all the
operations of nature carried on by an opposition of principles, of

25. [The ancient Manichean view was that the world is run by both a good force
and an evil one.]

hot and cold, moist and dry, light and heavy? The true conclusion is that the original source of all things is entirely indifferent to all these principles, and has no more regard to good above ill than to heat above cold, or to drought above moisture, or to light above heavy.

There may *four* hypotheses be framed concerning the first causes of the universe: *that* they are endowed with perfect goodness; *that* they have perfect malice; *that* they are opposite and have both goodness and malice; *that* they have neither goodness nor malice. Mixed phenomena can never prove the two former unmixed principles; and the uniformity and steadiness of general laws seem to oppose the third. The fourth, therefore, seems by far the most probable.

What I have said concerning natural evil will apply to moral with little or no variation; and we have no more reason to infer that the rectitude of the Supreme Being resembles human rectitude than that his benevolence resembles the human. Nay, it will be thought that we have still greater cause to exclude from him moral sentiments, such as we feel them; since moral evil, in the opinion of many, is much more predominant above moral good than natural evil above natural good.

But even though this should not be allowed, and though the virtue which is in mankind should be acknowledged much superior to the vice; yet, so long as there is any vice at all in the universe, it will very much puzzle you anthropomorphites how to account for it. You must assign a cause for it, without having recourse to the first cause. But as every effect must have a cause, and that cause another, you must either carry on the progression *in infinitum*, or rest on that original principle, who is the ultimate cause of all things. . . .

Demea: Hold! hold! cried *Demea:* Whither does your imagination hurry you? I joined in alliance with you in order to prove the incomprehensible nature of the Divine Being, and refute the principles of *Cleanthes*, who would measure everything by human rule and standard. But I now find you running into all the topics of the greatest libertines and infidels, and betraying that holy cause which you seemingly espoused. Are you secretly, then, a more dangerous enemy than *Cleanthes* himself?

Cleanthes: And are you so late in perceiving it? replied *Cleanthes.* Believe me, *Demea,* your friend *Philo,* from the beginning, has been amusing himself at both our expense; and it must be confessed that the injudicious reasoning of our vulgar theology has given him but too just a handle of ridicule. The total infirmity of human reason, the absolute incomprehensibility of the Divine Nature, the great and universal misery, and still greater wickedness of men; these are strange topics, surely, to be so fondly cherished by orthodox divines and doctors. In ages of stupidity and ignorance, indeed, these principles may safely be espoused; and perhaps no views of things are more proper to promote superstition than such as encourage the blind amazement, the diffidence, and melancholy of mankind. But at present...

Philo: Blame not so much, interposed *Philo*, the ignorance of these reverend gentlemen. They know how to change their style with the times. Formerly, it was a most popular theological topic to maintain that human life was vanity and misery, and to exaggerate all the ills and pains which are incident to men. But of late years, divines, we find, begin to retract this position and maintain, though still with some hesitation, that there are more goods than evils, more pleasures than pains, even in this life. When religion stood entirely upon temper and education, it was thought proper to encourage melancholy; as, indeed, mankind never have recourse to superior powers so readily as in that disposition. But as men have now learned to form principles and to draw consequences, it is necessary to change the batteries, and to make use of such arguments as will endure at least some scrutiny and examination. This variation is the same (and from the same causes) with that which I formerly remarked with regard to skepticism.

Thus *Philo* continued to the last his spirit of opposition, and his censure of established opinions. But I could observe that *Demea* did not at all relish the latter part of the discourse; and he took occasion soon after, on some pretence or other, to leave the company.

Part XII

After *Demea's* departure, *Cleanthes* and *Philo* continued the conversation in the following manner. **Cleanthes:** Our friend, I am afraid, said *Cleanthes*, will have little inclination to revive this topic of discourse while you are in company; and to tell the truth, *Philo*, I should rather wish to reason with either of you apart on a subject so sublime and interesting. Your spirit of controversy, joined to your abhorrence of vulgar superstition, carries you strange lengths when engaged in an argument; and there is nothing so sacred and venerable, even in your own eyes, which you spare on that occasion.

Philo: I must confess, replied *Philo*, that I am less cautious on the subject of Natural Religion than on any other; both because I know that I can never, on that head, corrupt the principles of any man of common sense and because no one, I am confident, in whose eyes I appear a man of common sense will ever mistake my intentions. You, in particular, *Cleanthes*, with whom I live in unreserved intimacy; you are sensible that, notwithstanding the freedom of my conversation and my love of singular arguments, no one has a deeper sense of religion impressed on his mind, or pays more profound adoration to the Divine Being, as he discovers himself to reason in the inexplicable contrivance and artifice of nature. A purpose, an intention, a design strikes everywhere the most careless, the most stupid thinker; and no man can be so hardened in absurd systems as at all times to reject it. *That nature does nothing in vain* is a maxim established in all the Schools, merely from the contemplation of the works of nature, without any religious purpose; and, from a firm conviction of its truth, an anatomist who had observed a new organ or canal would never be satisfied till he had also discovered its use and intention. One great foundation of the *Copernican* system is the maxim *that nature acts by the simplest methods, and chooses the most proper means to any end;* and astronomers often, without thinking of it, lay this strong foundation of piety and religion. The same thing is observable in other parts of philosophy; and thus all the sciences almost lead us insensibly to acknowledge a first intelligent Author; and their authority is often so much the greater as they do not directly profess that intention.

It is with pleasure I hear *Galen* reason concerning the structure of the human body. The anatomy of a man, says he,[26] discovers above 600 different muscles; and whoever duly considers these will find that, in each of them, nature must have adjusted at least ten different circumstances in order to attain the end which she proposed: proper figure, just magnitude, right disposition of the several ends, upper and lower position of the whole, the due insertion of the several nerves, veins, and arteries; so that, in the muscles alone, above 6000 several views and intentions must have been formed and executed. The bones he calculates to be 284: The distinct purposes aimed at in the structure of each, above forty. What a prodigious display of artifice, even in these simple and homogeneous parts! But if we consider the skin, ligaments, vessels, glandules, humors, the several limbs and members of the body; how must our astonishment rise upon us, in proportion to the number and intricacy of the parts so artificially adjusted! The further we advance in these researches, we discover new scenes of art and wisdom; but descry still, at a distance, further scenes beyond our reach; in the fine internal structure of the parts, in the economy of the brain, in the fabric of the seminal vessels. All these artifices are repeated in every different species of animal, with wonderful variety, and with exact propriety, suited to the different intentions of nature in framing each species. And if the infidelity of *Galen*, even when these natural sciences were still imperfect, could not withstand such striking appearances, to what pitch of pertinacious obstinacy must a philosopher in this age have attained who can now doubt of a Supreme Intelligence!

Could I meet with one of this species (who, I thank God, are very rare), I would ask him: Supposing there were a God who did not discover himself immediately to our senses, were it possible for him to give stronger proofs of his existence than what appear on the whole face of nature? What indeed could such a Divine Being do but copy the present economy of things; render many of his artifices so plain that no stupidity could mistake them; afford glimpses of still greater artifices which demonstrate his prodigious superiority

26. *De Formatione Foetus.* [Galen was the most reknowned physician of antiquity. He died around A.D. 199, and left voluminous medical writings.]

above our narrow apprehensions, and conceal altogether a great many from such imperfect creatures? Now, according to all rules of just reasoning, every fact must pass for undisputed when it is supported by all the arguments which its nature admits of, even though these arguments be not, in themselves, very numerous or forcible: How much more in the present case where no human imagination can compute their number, and no understanding estimate their cogency.

Cleanthes: I shall further add, said *Cleanthes*, to what you have so well urged, that one great advantage of the principle of theism is that it is the only system of cosmogony which can be rendered intelligible and complete, and yet can throughout preserve a strong analogy to what we every day see and experience in the world. The comparison of the universe to a machine of human contrivance is so obvious and natural, and is justified by so many instances of order and design in nature, that it must immediately strike all unprejudiced apprehensions, and procure universal approbation. Whoever attempts to weaken this theory cannot pretend to succeed by establishing in its place any other that is precise and determinate: It is sufficient for him if he start doubts and difficulties; and, by remote and abstract views of things, reach that suspense of judgment which is here the utmost boundary of his wishes. But, besides that this state of mind is in itself unsatisfactory, it can never be steadily maintained against such striking appearances as continually engage us into the religious hypothesis. A false, absurd system, human nature, from the force of prejudice, is capable of adhering to with obstinacy and perseverance; but no system at all, in opposition to a theory supported by strong and obvious reason, by natural propensity, and by early education, I think it absolutely impossible to maintain or defend.

Philo: So little, replied *Philo*, do I esteem this suspense of judgment in the present case to be possible that I am apt to suspect there enters somewhat of a dispute of words into this controversy, more than is usually imagined. That the works of nature bear a great analogy to the productions of art is evident; and, according to all the rules of good reasoning, we ought to infer, if we argue at all concerning them, that their causes have a proportional analogy. But as there are also considerable differences, we have reason to suppose a proportional difference in the causes, and, in particular, ought to attribute a much higher degree of power and energy to the Supreme Cause than any we have ever observed in mankind. Here, then, the existence of a DEITY is plainly ascertained by reason; and if we make it a question whether, on account of these analogies, we can properly call him a *mind* or *intelligence*, notwithstanding the vast difference which may reasonably be supposed between him and human minds; what is this but a mere verbal controversy? No man can deny the analogies between the effects: to restrain ourselves from inquiring concerning the causes is scarcely possible. From this inquiry the legitimate conclusion is that the causes have also an analogy: And if we are not contented with calling the first and supreme cause a GOD or DEITY, but desire to vary the expression, what can we call him but MIND or THOUGHT, to which he is justly supposed to bear a considerable resemblance?

All men of sound reason are disgusted with verbal disputes, which abound so much in philosophical and theological inquiries; and it is found that the only remedy for this abuse must arise from clear definitions, from the precision of those ideas which enter into any argument, and from the strict and uniform use of those terms which are employed. But there is a species of controversy which, from the very nature of language and of human ideas, is involved in perpetual ambiguity, and can never, by any precaution or any definitions, be able to reach a reasonable certainty or precision. These are the controversies concerning the degrees of any quality or circumstance. Men may argue to all eternity whether *Hannibal* be a great, or a very great, or a superlatively great man, what degree of beauty *Cleopatra* possessed, what epithet of praise *Livy* or *Thucydides* is entitled to, without bringing the controversy to any determination. The disputants may here agree in their sense and differ in the terms, or *vice versa*, yet never be able to define their terms so as to enter into each other's meaning: Because the degrees of these qualities are not, like quantity or number, susceptible of any exact mensuration, which may be the standard in the controversy. That the dispute concerning theism is of this nature, and consequently is merely verbal, or, perhaps, if possible, still more incurably ambiguous, will appear upon the slightest inquiry. I ask the theist if he does not allow that there is a great and immeasurable, because incomprehensible, difference between the *human* and the *divine* mind: The more pious he is, the more readily will he assent to the affirmative, and the more will he be disposed to magnify the difference: He will even assert that the difference is of a nature which cannot be too much magnified. I next turn to the atheist, who, I assert, is only nominally so and can never possibly be in earnest; and I ask him whether, from the coherence and apparent sympathy in all the parts of this world, there be not a certain degree of analogy among all the operations of nature, in every situation and in every age; whether the rotting of a turnip, the generation of an animal, and the structure of human thought, be not energies that probably bear some remote analogy to each other: It is impossible he can deny it: He will readily acknowledge it. Having obtained this concession, I push him still further in his retreat, and I ask him if it be not probable that the principle which first arranged and still maintains order in this universe bears not also some remote inconceivable analogy to the other operations of nature and, among the rest, to the economy of human mind and thought. However reluctant, he must give his assent. Where then, cry I to both these antagonists, is the subject of your dispute? The theist allows that the original intelligence is very different from human reason: The atheist allows that the original principle of order bears some remote analogy to it. Will you quarrel, Gentlemen, about the degrees, and enter into a controversy which admits not of any precise meaning, nor consequently of any determination? If you should be so obstinate, I should not be surprised to find you insensibly change sides; while the theist, on the one hand, exaggerates the dissimilarity between the Supreme Being and frail, imperfect, variable, fleeting, and mortal creatures; and the atheist, on the other, magnifies the analogy among all the operations of nature, in every period, every situation, and every position. Consider then where the real point of controversy lies; and if you cannot lay aside your disputes, endeavor, at least, to cure yourselves of your animosity.

And here I must also acknowledge, *Cleanthes*, that, as the works of Nature have a much greater analogy to the effects of *our* art and contrivance than to those of *our* benevolence and justice; we have reason to infer that the natural attributes of the Deity have a greater resemblance to those of men than his moral have to human virtues. But what is the consequence? Nothing but this, that the moral qualities of man are more defective in their kind than his natural abilities. For, as the Supreme Being is allowed to be absolutely and entirely perfect, whatever differs most from him departs the farthest from the supreme standard of rectitude and perfection.[27]

---

27. It seems evident that the dispute between the skeptics and dogmatists is entirely verbal, or, at least, regards only the degrees of doubt and assurance which we ought to indulge with regard to all reasoning: and such disputes are commonly, at the bottom, verbal and admit not of any precise determination. No philosophical dogmatist denies that there are difficulties both with regard to the senses and to all science, and that these difficulties are, in a regular, logical method, absolutely in-

These, *Cleanthes,* are my unfeigned sentiments on this subject; and these sentiments, you know, I have ever cherished and maintained. But in proportion to my veneration for true religion is my abhorrence of vulgar superstitions; and I indulge a peculiar pleasure, I confess, in pushing such principles sometimes into absurdity, sometimes into impiety. And you are sensible that all bigots, notwithstanding their great aversion to the latter above the former, are commonly equally guilty of both.

Cleanthes: My inclination, replied *Cleanthes,* lies, I own, a contrary way. Religion, however corrupted, is still better than no religion at all. The doctrine of a future state is so strong and necessary a security to morals that we never ought to abandon or neglect it. For if finite and temporary rewards and punishments have so great an effect, as we daily find: How much greater must be expected from such as are infinite and eternal?

Philo: How happens it then, said *Philo,* if vulgar superstition be so salutary to society, that all history abounds so much with accounts of its pernicious consequences on public affairs? Factions, civil wars, persecutions, subversions of government, oppression, slavery: these are the dismal consequences which always attend its prevalence over the minds of men. If the religious spirit be ever mentioned in any historical narration, we are sure to meet afterwards with a detail of the miseries which attend it. And no period of time can be happier or more prosperous than those in which it is never regarded or heard of.

Cleanthes: The reason of this observation, replied *Cleanthes,* is obvious. The proper office of religion is to regulate the hearts of men, humanize their conduct, infuse the spirit of temperance, order, and obedience; and, as its operation is silent and only enforces the motives of morality and justice, it is in danger of being overlooked and confounded with these other motives. When it distinguishes itself, and acts as a separate principle over men, it has departed from its proper sphere and has become only a cover to faction and ambition.

Philo: And so will all religion, said *Philo,* except the

---

solvable. No skeptic denies that we lie under an absolute necessity, notwithstanding these difficulties, of thinking, and believing, and reasoning, with regard to all kinds of subjects, and even of frequently assenting with confidence and security. The only difference, then, between these sects, if they merit that name, is that the skeptic, from habit, caprice, or inclination, insists most on the difficulties; the dogmatist, for like reasons, on the necessity.

philosophical and rational kind. Your reasonings are more easily eluded than my facts. The inference is not just, because finite and temporary rewards and punishments have so great influence that therefore such as are infinite and eternal must have so much greater. Consider, I beseech you, the attachment which we have to present things, and the little concern which we discover for objects so remote and uncertain. When divines are declaiming against the common behavior and conduct of the world, they always represent this principle as the strongest imaginable (which indeed it is), and describe almost all human kind as lying under the influence of it, and sunk into the deepest lethargy and unconcern about their religious interests. Yet these same divines, when they refute their speculative antagonists, suppose the motives of religion to be so powerful that, without them, it were impossible for civil society to subsist; nor are they ashamed of so palpable a contradiction. It is certain, from experience, that the smallest grain of natural honesty and benevolence has more effect on men's conduct than the most pompous views suggested by theological theories and systems. A man's natural inclination works incessantly upon him; it is forever present to the mind, and mingles itself with every view and consideration: whereas religious motives, where they act at all, operate only by starts and bounds; and it is scarcely possible for them to become altogether habitual to the mind. The force of the greatest gravity, say the philosophers, is infinitely small, in comparison of that of the least impulse, yet it is certain that the smallest gravity will, in the end, prevail above a great impulse because no strokes or blows can be repeated with such constancy as attraction and gravitation.

Another advantage of inclination: It engages on its side all the wit and ingenuity of the mind, and, when set in opposition to religious principles, seeks every method and art of eluding them; in which it is almost always successful. Who can explain the heart of man, or account for those strange salvos and excuses with which people satisfy themselves when they follow their inclinations in opposition to their religious duty? This is well understood in the world; and none but fools ever repose less trust in a man because they hear that, from study and philosophy, he has entertained some speculative doubts with regard to theological subjects. And when we have to do with a man who makes a great profession of religion and devotion, has this any other effect upon several who pass for prudent than to put them on their guard, lest they be cheated and deceived by him?

We must further consider that philosophers, who cultivate reason and reflection, stand less in need of such motives to keep them under the restraint of morals: And that the vulgar, who alone may need them, are utterly incapable of so pure a religion as represents the Deity to be pleased with nothing but virtue in human behavior. The recommendations to the Divinity are generally supposed to be either frivolous observances or rapturous ecstasies or a bigoted credulity. We need not run back into antiquity or wander into remote regions to find instances of this degeneracy. Amongst ourselves, some have been guilty of that atrociousness, unknown to the Egyptian and Grecian superstitions, of declaiming, in express terms, against morality, and representing it as a sure forfeiture of the divine favor if the least trust or reliance be laid upon it.

But even though superstition or enthusiasm should not put itself in direct opposition to morality; the very diverting of the attention, the raising up a new and frivolous species of merit, the preposterous distribution which it makes of praise and blame, must have the most pernicious consequences, and weaken extremely men's attachment to the natural motives of justice and humanity.

Such a principle of action likewise, not being any of the familiar motives of human conduct, acts only by intervals on the temper, and must be roused by continual efforts in order to render the pious zealot satisfied with his own conduct and make him fulfil his devotional task. Many religious exercises are entered into with seeming fervor where the heart, at the time, feels cold and languid. A habit of dissimulation is by degrees contracted: And fraud and falsehood become the predominant principle. Hence the reason of that vulgar observation that the highest zeal in religion and the deepest hypocrisy, so far from being inconsistent, are often or commonly united in the same individual character.

The bad effects of such habits, even in common life, are easily imagined: But, where the interests of religion are concerned, no morality can be forcible enough to bind the enthusiastic zealot. The sacredness of the cause sanctifies every measure which can be made use of to promote it.

The steady attention alone to so important an interest as that of eternal salvation is apt to extinguish the benevolent affections, and beget a narrow, contracted selfishness. And when such a temper is encouraged, it easily eludes all the general precepts of charity and benevolence.

Thus the motives of vulgar superstition have no great influence on general conduct, nor is the operation favorable to morality, in the instances where they predominate.

Is there any maxim in politics more certain and infallible than that both the number and authority of priests should be confined within very narrow limits, and that the civil magistrate ought, for ever, to keep his *fasces* and *axes* from such dangerous hands? But if the spirit of popular religion were so salutary to society, a contrary maxim ought to prevail. The greater number of priests and their greater authority and riches will always augment the religious spirit. And though the priests have the guidance of this spirit, why may we not expect a superior sanctity of life and greater benevolence and moderation from persons who are set apart for religion, who are continually inculcating it upon others, and who must themselves imbibe a greater share of it? Whence comes it then that, in fact, the utmost a wise magistrate can propose with regard to popular religions is, as far as possible, to make a saving game of it, and to prevent their pernicious consequences with regard to society? Every expedient which he tries for so humble a purpose is surrounded with inconveniences. If he admits only one religion among his subjects, he must sacrifice, to an uncertain prospect of tranquillity, every consideration of public liberty, science, reason, industry, and even his own independence. If he gives indulgence to several sects, which is the wiser maxim, he must preserve a very philosophical indifference to all of them and carefully restrain the pretensions of the prevailing sect; otherwise he can expect nothing but endless disputes, quarrels, factions, persecutions, and civil commotions.

True religion, I allow, has no such pernicious consequences: But we must treat of religion as it has commonly been found in the world; nor have I anything to do with that speculative tenet of theism which, as it is a species of philosophy, must partake of the beneficial influence of that principle, and, at the same time, must lie under a like inconvenience of being always confined to very few persons.

Oaths are requisite in all courts of judicature, but it is a question whether their authority arises from any popular religion. It is the solemnity and importance of the occasion, the regard to reputation, and the reflecting on the general interests of society, which are the chief restraints upon mankind. Customhouse oaths and political oaths are but little regarded even by some who pretend to principles of honesty and religion: And a *Quaker's* asseveration is with us justly put upon the same footing with the oath of any other person. I know that *Polybius*[28] ascribes the infamy of Greek faith to the prevalence of the *Epicurean* philosophy; but I know also that Punic faith had as bad a reputation in ancient times as Irish evidence has in modern, though we cannot account for these vulgar observations by the same reason. Not to mention that Greek faith was infamous before the rise of the *Epicurean* philosophy; and *Euripides*,[29] in a passage which I shall point out to you, has glanced a remarkable stroke of satire against his nation, with regard to this circumstance.

Cleanthes: Take care, *Philo*, replied *Cleanthes*, take care; push not matters too far, allow not your zeal against false religion to undermine your veneration for the true. Forfeit not this principle, the chief, the only great comfort in life and our principal support amidst all the attacks of adverse fortune. The most agreeable reflection which it is possible for human imagination to suggest is that of genuine theism, which represents us as the workmanship of a Being perfectly good, wise, and powerful; who created us for happiness; and who, having implanted in us immeasurable desires of good, will prolong our existence to all eternity, and will transfer us into an infinite variety of scenes, in order to satisfy those desires and render our felicity complete and durable. Next to such a Being himself (if the comparison be allowed), the happiest lot which we can imagine is that of being under his guardianship and protection.

Philo: These appearances, said Philo, are most engaging and alluring; and, with regard to the true philosopher, they are more than appearances. But it happens here, as in the former case, that, with regard to the greater part of mankind, the appearances are deceitful, and that the terrors of religion commonly prevail above its comforts.

It is allowed that men never have recourse to devotion so readily as when dejected with grief or depressed with sickness. Is not this a proof that the religious spirit is not so nearly allied to joy as to sorrow?

Cleanthes: But men, when afflicted, find consolation in religion, replied *Cleanthes*. **Philo:**   Sometimes, said *Philo*; but it is natural to imagine that they will form a notion of those unknown beings, suitable to the present gloom and melancholy of their temper, when they betake themselves to the contemplation of them. Accordingly, we find the tremendous images to predominate in all

28. [Polybius, *The Histories*, Book VI, chap. 54.]

29. *Iphigenia in Tauris.*

religions; and we ourselves, after having employed the most exalted expression in our descriptions of the Deity, fall into the flattest contradiction in affirming that the damned are infinitely superior in number to the elect.

I shall venture to affirm that there never was a popular religion which represented the state of departed souls in such a light as would render it eligible for human kind that there should be such a state. These fine models of religion are the mere product of philosophy. For as death lies between the eye and the prospect of futurity, that event is so shocking to nature that it must throw a gloom on all the regions which lie beyond it; and suggest to the generality of mankind the idea of *Cerberus* and *Furies*, devils, and torrents of fire and brimstone.

It is true, both fear and hope enter into religion because both these passions, at different times, agitate the human mind, and each of them forms a species of divinity suitable to itself. But when a man is in a cheerful disposition, he is fit for business, or company, or entertainment of any kind; and he naturally applies himself to these and thinks not of religion. When melancholy and dejected, he has nothing to do but brood upon the terrors of the invisible world, and to plunge himself still deeper in affliction. It may indeed happen that, after he has, in this manner, engraved the religious opinions deep into his thought and imagination, there may arrive a change of health or circumstances which may restore his good humor and, raising cheerful prospects of futurity, make him run into the other extreme of joy and triumph. But still it must be acknowledged that, as terror is the primary principle of religion, it is the passion which always predominates in it, and admits but of short intervals of pleasure.

Not to mention that these fits of excessive, enthusiastic joy, by exhausting the spirits, always prepare the way for equal fits of superstitious terror and dejection; nor is there any state of mind so happy as the calm and equable. But this state it is impossible to support where a man thinks that he lies in such profound darkness and uncertainty, between an eternity of happiness and an eternity of misery. No wonder that such an opinion disjoints the ordinary frame of the mind and throws it into the utmost confusion. And though that opinion is seldom so steady in its operation as to influence all the actions; yet it is apt to make a considerable breach in the temper, and to produce that gloom and melancholy so remarkable in all devout people.

It is contrary to common sense to entertain apprehensions or terrors upon account of any opinion whatsoever, or to imagine that we run any risk hereafter, by the freest use of our reason. Such a sentiment implies both an *absurdity* and an *inconsistency*. It is an absurdity to believe that the Deity has human passions, and one of the lowest of human passions, a restless appetite for applause. It is an inconsistency to believe that, since the Deity has this human passion, he has not others also; and, in particular, a disregard to the opinions of creatures so much inferior.

To know God, says *Seneca, is to worship him.* All other worship is indeed absurd, superstitious, and even impious. It degrades him to the low condition of mankind, who are delighted with entreaty, solicitation, presents, and flattery. Yet is this impiety the smallest of which superstition is guilty. Commonly, it depresses the Deity far below the condition of mankind, and represents him as a capricious demon who exercises his power without reason and without humanity! And were that Divine Being disposed to be offended at the vices and follies of silly mortals, who are his own workmanship, ill would it surely fare with the votaries of most popular superstitions. Nor would any of human race merit his *favor* but a very few, the philosophical theists, who entertain or rather indeed endeavor to entertain suitable notions of his divine perfections. As the only persons entitled to his *compassion* and *indulgence* would be the philosophical skeptics, a sect almost equally rare, who, from a natural diffidence of their own capacity, suspend or endeavor to suspend all judgment with regard to such sublime and such extraordinary subjects.

If the whole of natural theology, as some people seem to maintain, resolves itself into one simple, though somewhat ambiguous, at least undefined, proposition, *That the cause or causes of order in the universe probably bear some remote analogy to human intelligence:* If this proposition be not capable of extension, variation, or more particular explication: If it affords no inference that affects human life, or can be the source of any action or forbearance: And if the analogy, imperfect as it is, can be carried no further than to the human intelligence, and cannot be transferred, with any appearance of probability, to the other qualities of the mind: If this really be the case, what can the most inquisitive, contemplative, and religious man do more than give a plain, philosophical assent to the proposition, as often as it occurs, and believe that the arguments on which it is established exceed the objections which lie against it?

Some astonishment, indeed, will naturally arise from the greatness of the object: Some melancholy from its obscurity: Some contempt of human reason that it can give no solution more satisfactory with regard to so extraordinary and magnificent a question. But believe me, *Cleanthes*, the most natural sentiment which a well-disposed mind will feel on this occasion is a longing desire and expectation that heaven would be pleased to dissipate, at least alleviate, this profound ignorance by affording some more particular revelation to mankind, and making discoveries of the nature, attributes, and operations of the divine object of our faith. A person, seasoned with a just sense of the imperfections of natural reason, will fly to revealed truth with the greatest avidity: While the haughty dogmatist, persuaded that he can erect a complete system of theology by the mere help of philosophy, disdains any further aid and rejects this adventitious instructor. To be a philosophical skeptic is, in a man of letters, the first and most essential step towards being a sound, believing *Christian*—a proposition which I would willingly recommend to the attention of Pamphilus; and I hope *Cleanthes* will forgive me for interposing so far in the education and instruction of his pupil.

Pamphilus: *Cleanthes* and *Philo* pursued not this conversation much further; and as nothing ever made greater impression on me than all the reasonings of that day; so I confess that, upon a serious review of the whole, I cannot but think that *Philo's* principles are more probable than *Demea's*, but that those of *Cleanthes* approach still nearer to the truth.

UNPUBLISHED ESSAYS

ESSAY I—Of the Immortality of the Soul

By the mere light of reason it seems difficult to prove the Immortality of the Soul. The arguments for it are commonly derived either from *metaphysical* topics, or *moral, or physical.* But in reality, it is the gospel, and the gospel alone, that has brought life and immortality to light.

I. Metaphysical topics are founded on the supposition that the soul is immaterial, and that it is impossible for thought to belong to a material substance.

But just metaphysics teach us, that the notion of substance is wholly confused and imperfect, and that we have no other idea of any substance, than as an aggregate of particular qualities inhering in an unknown something. Matter, therefore, and spirit, are at bottom equally unknown; and we cannot determine what qualities may inhere in the one or in the other.

They likewise teach us, that nothing can be decided *a priori* concerning any cause or effect; and that experience, being the only source of our judgments of this nature, we cannot know from any other principle, whether matter, by its structure or arrangement, may not be the cause of thought. Abstract reasonings cannot decide any question of fact or existence.

But admitting a spiritual substance to be dispersed throughout the universe, like the ethereal fire of the *Stoics,* and to be the only inherent subject of thought, we have reason to conclude from *analogy,* that nature uses it after the manner she does the other substance, matter. She employs it as a kind of paste or clay; modifies it into a variety of forms and existences; dissolves after a time each modification, and from its substance erects a new form. As the same material substance may successively compose the bodies of all animals, the same spiritual substance may compose their minds: Their consciousness, or that system of thought, which they formed during life, may be continually dissolved by death; and nothing interest them in the new modification. The most positive assertors of the mortality of the soul, never denied the immortality of its substance. And that an immaterial substance, as well as a material, may lose its memory or consciousness, appears, in part, from experience, if the soul be immaterial.

Reasoning from the common course of nature, and without supposing any *new* interposition of the supreme cause, which ought always to be excluded from philosophy; what is incorruptible must also be ingenerable. The soul, therefore, if immortal, existed before our birth: And if the former existence nowise concerned us, neither will the latter.

Animals undoubtedly feel, think, love, hate, will, and even reason, though in a more imperfect manner than man. Are their souls also immaterial and immortal?

II. Let us now consider the *moral* arguments, chiefly those arguments derived from the justice of God, which is supposed to be further interested in the further punishment of the vicious and reward of the virtuous.

But these arguments are grounded on the supposition, that God has attributes beyond what he has exerted in this universe, with which alone we are acquainted. Whence do we infer the existence of these attributes?

It is very safe for us to affirm, that, whatever we know the deity to have actually done, is best; but it is very dangerous to affirm, that he must always do what to us seems best. In how many instances would this reasoning fail us with regard to the present world.

But if any purpose of nature be clear, we may affirm, that the whole scope and intention of man's creation, so far as we can judge by natural reason, is limited to the present life. With how weak a concern, from the original, inherent structure of the mind and passions, does he ever look further? What comparison either for steadiness or efficacy, between so floating an idea, and the most doubtful persuasion of any matter of fact, that occurs in common life?

There arise, indeed, in some minds, some unaccountable terrors with regard to futurity: But these would quickly vanish, were they not artificially fostered by precept and education. And those, who foster them: what is their motive? Only to gain a livelihood, and to acquire power and riches in this world. Their very zeal and industry, therefore, are an argument against them.

What cruelty, what iniquity, what injustice in nature, to confine thus all our concern, as well as all our knowledge, to the present life, if there be another scene still waiting us, of infinitely greater consequence? Ought this barbarous deceit to be ascribed to a beneficent and wise being?

Observe with what exact proportion the task to be performed, and the performing powers, are adjusted throughout all nature. If the reason of man gives him a great superiority above other animals, his necessities are proportionably multiplied upon him. His whole time, his whole capacity, activity, courage, passion, find sufficient employment, in fencing against the miseries of his present condition. And frequently, nay almost always, are too slender for the business assigned them.

A pair of shoes, perhaps, was never yet wrought to the highest degree of perfection, which that commodity is capable of attaining. Yet it is necessary, at least very useful, that there should be some politicians and moralists, even some geometers, historians, poets, and philosophers among mankind.

The powers of men are no more superior to their wants, considered merely in this life, than those of foxes and hares are, compared to *their* wants and to *their* period of existence. The inference from parity of reason is therefore obvious.

On the theory of the soul's mortality, the inferiority of women's capacity is easily accounted for: Their domestic life requires no higher faculties either of mind or body. This circumstance vanishes and becomes absolutely insignificant, on the religious theory: The one sex has an equal task to perform with the other: Their powers of reason and resolution ought also to have been equal, and both of them infinitely greater than at present.

As every effect implies a cause, and that another, till we reach the first cause of all, which is the *Deity*; every thing that happens, is ordained by him; and nothing can be the object of his punishment or vengeance.

By what rule are punishments and rewards distributed? What is the Divine standard of merit and demerit? Shall we Suppose, that human sentiments have place in the Deity? However bold that hypothesis, We have no conception of any other sentiments.

According to human sentiments, sense, courage, good manners, industry, prudence, genius, &c. are essential parts of personal merits. Shall we therefore erect an elysium for poets and heroes, like that of the ancient mythology? Why confine all rewards to one species of virtue?

Punishment, without any proper end or purpose, is inconsistent with *our* ideas of goodness and justice; and no end can be served by it after the whole scene is closed.

Punishment, according to *our* conception, should bear some proportion to the offence. Why then eternal punishment for the temporary offences of so frail a creature as man? Can any one approve of *Alexander's* rage, who intended to exterminate a whole nation, because they had seized his favourite horse, Bucephalus?[1]

Heaven and hell suppose two distinct species of men, the good and the bad. But the greatest part of mankind float between vice and virtue.

Were one to go round the world with an intention of giving a good supper to the righteous and a sound drubbing to the wicked, he would frequently be embarassed in his choice, and would find, that the merits and demerits of most men and women scarcely amount to the value of either.

To suppose measures of approbation and blame, different from the human, confounds every thing. Whence do we learn, that there is such a thing as moral distinctions, but from our own sentiments?

What man, who has not met with personal provocation (or what good-natur'd man who has), could inflict on crimes, from the sense of blame alone, even the common, legal, frivolous punishments? And does any thing steel the breast of judges and juries against the sentiments of humanity but reflections on necessity and public interest?

By the Roman law, those who had been guilty of parricide, and confessed their crime, were put into a sack, along with an ape, a dog, and a serpent; and thrown into the river: Death alone was the punishment of those, who denied their guilt, however fully proved. A criminal was tried before *Augustus*, and condemned after a full conviction: but the humane emperor, when he put the last interrogatory, gave it such a turn as to lead the wretch into a denial of his guilt. *"You surely*, said the prince, *did not kill your father?"*[2] This lenity suits our natural ideas of RIGHT, even towards the greatest of all criminals, and even though it prevents so inconsiderable a sufferance. Nay, even the most bigoted priest would naturally, without reflection, approve of it; provided the crime was not heresy or infidelity. For as these crimes hurt himself in his *temporal* interest and advantages; perhaps he may not be altogether so indulgent to them.

The chief source of moral ideas is the reflection on the interests of human society. Ought these interests, so short, so frivolous, to be guarded by punishments, eternal and infinite? The damnation of one man is an infinitely greater evil in the universe, than the subver-

1. Quint. Curtis. lib. vi. cap. 5.
2. Suetonius, *Life of Augustus*, chap. 33.

sion of a thousand millions of kingdoms.

Nature has rendered human infancy peculiarly frail and mortal; as it were on purpose to refute the notion of a probationary state. The half of mankind die before they are rational creatures.

III. The *physical* arguments from the analogy of nature are strong for the mortality of the soul: and these are really the only philosophical arguments, which ought to be admitted with regard to this question, or indeed any question of fact.

Where any two objects are so closely connected, that all alterations, which we have ever seen in the one, are attended with proportionable alterations in the other: we ought to conclude, by all rules of analogy, that, when there are still greater alterations produced in the former, and it is totally dissolved, there follows a total dissolution of the latter.

Sleep, a very small effect on the body, is attended with a temporary extinction: at least, a great confusion in the soul.

The weakness of the body and that of the mind in infancy are exactly proportioned; their vigour in manhood, their sympathetic disorder in sickness, their common gradual decay in old age. The step further seems unavoidable; their common dissolution in death.

The last symptoms, which the mind discovers, are disorder, weakness, insensibility, and stupidity; the forerunners of its annihilation. The further progress of the same causes, encreasing the same effects, totally extinguish it.

Judging by the usual analogy of nature, no form can continue, when transferred to a condition of life very different from the original one, in which it was placed. Trees perish in the water; fishes in the air; animals in the earth. Even so small a difference as that of climate is often fatal. What reason then to imagine, that an immense alteration, such as is made on the soul by the dissolution of its body, and all its organs of thought and sensation, can be effected without the dissolution of the whole?

Every thing is in common between soul and body. The organs of the one are all of them the organs of the other. The existence therefore of the one must be dependent on the other.

The souls of animals are allowed to be mortal: and these bear so near a resemblance to the souls of men, that the analogy from one to the other forms a very strong argument. Their bodies are not more resembling: yet no one rejects the argument drawn from comparative anatomy. The *Metempsychosis* is therefore the only system of this kind, that philosophy can so much as hearken to.

Nothing in this world is perpetual. Every thing, however seemingly firm, is in continual flux and change: The world itself gives symptoms of frailty and dissolution: How contrary to analogy, therefore, to imagine, that one single form, seeming the frailest of any, and from the objects and causes subject to the greatest disorders, is immortal and indissoluble? What a daring theory is that! How lightly, not to say how rashly, entertained!

How to dispose of the infinite number of posthumous existences ought also to embarrass the religious theory. Every planet, in every solar system, we are at liberty to imagine peopled with intelligent, mortal beings: At least we can fix on no other supposition. For these, then, a new universe must, every generation, be created beyond the bounds of the present universe: or one must have been created at first so prodigiously wide as to admit of this continual influx of beings. Ought such bold suppositions to be received by any philosophy: and that merely on the pretext of a bare possibility?

When it is asked, whether *Agamemnon, Thersites, Hannibal, Nero,* and every stupid clown, that ever existed in *Italy, Scythia, Bactria,* or *Guinea,* are now alive; can any man think, that a scrutiny of nature will furnish arguments strong enough to answer so strange a question in the affirmative? The want of argument, without revelation, sufficiently establishes the negative.

But how much easier, says Pliny, and safer for each to trust in himself, and for us to derive our idea of future tranquility from our experience of it before birth![3] Our insensibility, before the composition of the body, seems to natural reason a proof of a like state after dissolution.

Were our horrors of annihilation an original passion, not the effect of our general love of happiness, it would rather prove the mortality of the soul: For as nature does nothing in vain, she would never give us a horror against an impossible event. She may give us a horror against an unavoidable event, provided our endeavours, as in the present case, may often remove it to some distance. Death is in the end unavoidable; yet the human species could not be preserved, had not nature inspired us with an aversion towards it.

All doctrines are to be suspected which are favoured by our passions. And the hopes and fears which give rise to this doctrine, are very obvious.

It is an infinite advantage in every controversy, to defend the negative. If the question be out of the common experienced course of nature, this circumstance is almost, if not altogether, decisive. By what arguments or analogies can we prove any state of existence, which no one ever saw, and which no wise resembles any that ever

---

3. Book VII, chap. 56.

was seen? Who will repose such trust in any pretended philosophy, as to admit upon its testimony the reality of so marvellous a scene? Some new species of logic is requisite for that purpose; and some new faculties of the mind, that they may enable us to comprehend that logic.

Nothing could set in a fuller light the infinite obligations which mankind have to divine revelation; since we find, that no other medium could ascertain this great and important truth.

ESSAY II—Of Suicide

One considerable advantage that arises from Philosophy, consists in the sovereign antidote which it affords to superstition and false religion. All other remedies against that pestilent distemper are vain, or, at least uncertain. Plain good sense and the practice of the world, which alone serve most purposes of life, are here found ineffectual: History as well as daily, experience affords instances of men endowed with the strongest capacity for business and affairs, who have all their lives crouched under slavery to the grossest superstition. Even gaiety and sweetness of temper, which infuse a balm into every other wound, afford no remedy to so virulent a poison; as we may particularly observe of the fair sex, who, tho' commonly possessed of these rich presents of nature, feel many of their joys blasted by this importunate intruder. But when sound philosophy has once gained possession of the mind, superstition is effectually excluded; and one may safely affirm, that her triumph over this enemy is more complete than over most of the vices and imperfections incident to human nature. Love or anger, ambition or avarice, have their root in the temper and affections, which the soundest reason is scarce ever able fully to correct. But superstition being founded on false opinion, must immediately vanish when true philosophy has inspired juster sentiments of superior powers. The contest is here more equal between the distemper and the medicine: And nothing can hinder the latter from proving effectual, but its being false and sophisticated.

It will here be superfluous to magnify the merits of philosophy, by displaying the pernicious tendency of that vice, of which it cures the human mind. The superstitious man, says Tully, is miserable in every scene, in every incident of life. Even sleep itself, which banishes all other cares of unhappy mortals, affords to him matter of new terror; while he examines his dreams, and finds in those visions of the night prognostications of future calamities. I may add, that tho' death alone can put a full period to his misery, he dares not fly to this refuge, but still prolongs a miserable existence from a vain fear, lest he offend his maker, by using the power, with which that beneficent being has endowed him. The presents of God and Nature are ravished from us by this cruel enemy; and notwithstanding that one step would remove us from the regions of pain and sorrow, her menaces still chain us down to a hated being, which she herself chiefly contributes to render miserable.

It is observed by such as have been reduced by the calamities of life to the necessity of employing this fatal remedy, that, if the unseasonable care of their friends deprive them of that species of death, which they proposed to themselves, they seldom venture upon any other, or can summon up so much resolution a second time, as to execute their purpose. So great is our horror of death, that when it presents itself, under any form, besides that to which a man has endeavoured to reconcile his imagination, it acquires new terrors and overcomes his feeble courage: But when the menaces of superstition are joined to this natural timidity, no wonder it quite deprives men of all power over their lives; since even many pleasures and enjoyments, to which we are carried by a strong propensity, are torn from us by this inhuman tyrant. Let us here endeavour to restore men to their native liberty by examining all the common arguments against Suicide, and shewing, that that action may be free from every imputation of guilt or blame, according to the sentiments of all the ancient philosophers.

If Suicide be criminal, it must be a transgression of our duty, either to God, our neighbour, or ourselves.

To prove that suicide is no transgression of our duty to God, the following considerations may perhaps suffice. In order to govern the material world, the almighty Creator has established general and immutable laws, by which all bodies, from the greatest planet to the smallest particle of matter, are maintained in their proper sphere and function. To govern the animal world, he has endowed all living creatures with bodily and mental powers; with senses, passions, appetites, memory and judgment; by which they are impelled or regulated in that course of life to which they are destined. These two distinct principles of the material and animal world, continually encroach upon each other, and mutually retard or forward each others operations. The powers of man and of all other animals are restrained and directed by the nature and qualities of the surrounding bodies; and the modifications and actions of these bodies are incessantly altered by the operation of all animals. Man is stopt by rivers in his passage over the surface of the earth; and rivers, when properly directed, lend their force to the motion of machines, which serve to the use of man. But tho' the provinces of the material and animal powers are not kept entirely separate, there result from thence no discord or disorder in the creation: On the contrary, from the mixture, union and contrast of all the various powers of inanimate bodies and living creatures, arises that surprizing harmony and proportion, which affords the surest argument of supreme wisdom.

The providence of the deity appears not immediately in any operation, but governs everything by those general and immutable laws, which have been established from the beginning of time. All events, in one sense, may be pronounced the action of the almighty; they all proceed from those powers with which he has endowed his creatures. A house which falls by its own weight is not brought to ruin by his providence more than one destroyed by the hands of men; nor are the human faculties less his workmanship, than the laws of motion and gravitation. When the passions play, when the judgment dictates, when the limbs obey; this is all the operation of God, and upon these animate principles, as well as upon the inanimate, has he established the government of the universe.

Every event is alike important in the eyes of that infinite being, who takes in at one glance the most distant regions of space and remotest periods of time. There is no event, however important to us, which he has exempted from the general laws that govern the universe, or which he has peculiarly reserved for his own immediate action and operation. The revolution of states and empires depends upon the smallest caprice or passion of single men; and the lives of men are shortened or extended by the smallest accident of air or diet, sunshine or tempest. Nature still continues her progress and operation; and if general laws be ever broke by particular volitions of the deity, 'tis after a manner which entirely escapes human observation. As, on the one hand, the elements and other inanimate parts of the creation carry on their action without regard to the particular interest and situation of men; so men are entrusted to their own judgment and discretion in the various shocks of matter, and may employ every faculty with which they are endowed, in order to provide for their ease, happiness, or preservation.

What is the meaning then of that principle, that a man who, tired of life, and hunted by pain and misery, bravely overcomes all the natural terrors of death and makes his escape from this cruel scene; that such a man, I say, has incurred the indignation of his creator by encroaching on the office of divine providence, and disturbing the order of the universe? Shall we assert that the Almighty has reserved to himself in any peculiar manner the disposal of the lives of men, and has not submitted that event, in common with others, to the general laws by which the universe is governed? This is plainly false. The lives of men depend upon the same laws as the lives of all other animals; and these are subjected to the general laws of matter and motion. The fall of a tower or the infusion of a poison will destroy a man equally with the meanest creature: An inundation sweeps away every thing without distinction that comes within the reach of its fury. Since therefore the lives of men are for ever dependent on the general laws of matter and motion, is a man's disposing of his life criminal, because in every case it is criminal to encroach upon these laws, or disturb their operation? But this seems absurd. All animals are entrusted to their own prudence and skill for their conduct in the world, and have full authority, as far as their power extends, to alter all the operations of nature. Without the exercise of this authority they could not subsist a moment. Every action, every motion of a man, innovates in the order of some parts of matter, and diverts from their ordinary course the general laws of motion. Putting together, therefore, these conclusions, we find *that* human life depends upon the general laws of matter and motion, and *that* it is no encroachment on the office of providence to disturb or alter these general laws. Has not every one, of consequence, the free disposal of his own life? And may he not lawfully employ that power with which nature has endowed him?

In order to destroy the evidence of this conclusion, we must shew a reason, why this particular case is excepted. Is it because human life is of so great importance, that it is a presumption for human prudence to dispose of it? But the life of a man is of no greater importance to the universe than that of an oyster. And were it of ever so great importance, the order of nature has actually submitted it to human prudence, and reduced us to a necessity in every incident of determining concerning it.

Were the disposal of human life so much reserved as the peculiar province of the almighty that it were an encroachment on his right for men to dispose of their own lives; it would be equally criminal to act for the preservation of life as for its destruction. If I turn aside a stone which is falling upon my head, I disturb the course of nature, and I invade the peculiar province of the almighty by lengthening out my life beyond the period which by the general laws of matter and motion he had assigned to it.

A hair, a fly, an insect is able to destroy this mighty being whose life is of such importance. Is it an absurdity to suppose that human prudence may lawfully dispose of what depends on such insignificant causes?

It would be no crime in me to divert the *Nile* or *Danube* from its course, were I able to effect such purposes. Where then is the crime of turning a few ounces of blood from their natural channel?

Do you imagine that I repine at providence or curse my creation, because I go out of life, and put a period to a being, which, were it to continue, would render me miserable? Far be such sentiments from me. I am only convinced of a matter of fact, which you yourself acknowledge possible, that human life may be unhappy, and that my existence, if further prolonged, would become uneligible. But I thank providence, both for the good which I have already enjoyed, and for the power with which I am endowed of escaping the ill that threatens me.[1] To you it belongs to repine at providence, who foolishly imagine that you have no such power, and who must still prolong a hated being, tho' loaded with pain and sickness, with shame and poverty.

Do you not teach, that when any ill befalls me, tho' by the malice of my enemies, I ought to be resigned to providence, and that the actions of men are the operations of the almighty as much as the actions of inanimate beings? When I fall upon my own sword, therefore, I receive my death equally from the hands of the Deity as if it had proceeded from a lion, a precipice, or a fever. The submission which you require to providence, in every calamity that befalls me, excludes not human skill and industry, if possibly by their means I can avoid or escape the calamity: And why may I not employ one remedy as well as another?

If my life be not my own, it were criminal for me to put it in danger, as well as to dispose of it: Nor could one man deserve the appellation of *Hero* whom glory or friendship transports into the greatest dangers, and another merit the reproach of *Wretch* or *Miscreant* who puts a period to his life from the same or like motives.

There is no being, which possesses any power or faculty, that it

---

1. SEN., Epist. 12. And let us thank God that no man can be kept in life. Seneca, *Epistles*, no. 12 [trans. by R.M. Gummere].

receives not from its creator, nor is there any one, which by ever so irregular an action can encroach upon the plan of his providence, or disorder the universe. Its operations are his works equally with that chain of events, which it invades, and which ever principle prevails; we may for that very reason conclude it to be most favoured by him. Be it animate, or inanimate, rational, or irrational; 'tis all a case: Its power is still derived from the supreme creator, and is alike comprehended in the order of his providence. When the horror of pain prevails over the love of life: When a voluntary action anticipates the effects of blind causes; it is only in consequence of those powers and principles, which he has implanted in his creatures. Divine providence is still inviolate and placed far beyond the reach of human injuries.[2]

'Tis impious, says the old *Roman* superstition, to divert rivers from their course, or invade the prerogatives of nature. 'Tis impious, says the *French* superstition, to inoculate for the small-pox, or usurp the business of providence, by voluntarily producing distempers and maladies. 'Tis impious, says the modern *European* superstition, to put a period to our own life, and thereby rebel against our creator; and why not impious, say I, to build houses, cultivate the ground, or sail upon the ocean? In all these actions we employ our powers of mind and body, to produce some innovation in the course of nature; and in none of them do we any more. They are all of them therefore equally innocent, or equally criminal.

But you are placed by providence, like a sentinel in a particular station, and when you desert it without being recalled, you are equally guilty of rebellion against your almighty sovereign, and have incurred his displeasure.—I ask, why do you conclude that providence has placed me in this station? For my part I find that I owe my birth to a long chain of causes, of which many and even the principal ones depended upon voluntary actions of men. *But Providence guided all these causes, and nothing happens in the universe without its consent and co-operation.* If so, then neither does my death, however voluntary, happen without its consent; and whenever pain or sorrow so far overcome my patience, as to make me tired of life, I may conclude that I am recalled from my station in the clearest and most express terms.

It is providence surely that has placed me at this present moment in this chamber: But may I not leave it when I think proper, without being liable to the imputation of having deserted my post or sta-

2. Tacitus, *Annals*, Book 1, 79.

tion? When I shall be dead, the principles of which I am composed will still perform their part in the universe, and will be equally useful in the grand fabric, as when they composed this individual creature. The difference to the whole will be no greater than betwixt my being in a chamber and in the open air. The one change is of more importance to me than the other; but not more so to the universe.

It is a kind of blasphemy to imagine that any created being can disturb the order of the world or invade the business of providence. It supposes, that that being possesses powers and faculties, which it received not from its creator, and which are not subordinate to his government and authority. A man may disturb society no doubt, and thereby incur the displeasure of the almighty: But the government of the world is placed far beyond his reach and violence. And how does it appear that the almighty is displeased with those actions that disturb society? By the principles which he has implanted in human nature, and which inspire us with a sentiment of remorse if we ourselves have been guilty of such actions, and with that of blame and disapprobation, if we ever observe them in others. Let us now examine, according to the method proposed, whether Suicide be of this kind of actions, and be a breach of our duty to our *neighbour* and to society.

A man, who retires from life, does no harm to society: He only ceases to do good; which, if it is an injury, is of the lowest kind.

All our obligations to do good to society seem to imply something reciprocal. I receive the benefits of society and therefore ought to promote its interests, but when I withdraw myself altogether from society, can I be bound any longer? But, allowing that our obligations to do good were perpetual, they have certainly some bounds; I am not obliged to do a small good to society at the expence of a great harm to myself. Why then should I prolong a miserable existence, because of some frivolous advantage which the public may perhaps receive from me? If upon account of age and infirmities I may lawfully resign any office, and employ my time altogether in fencing against these calamities, and alleviating as much as possible the miseries of my future life: Why may I not cut short these miseries at once by an action which is no more prejudicial to society?

But suppose that it is no longer in my power to promote the interest of the public; suppose that I am a burthen to it; suppose that my life hinders some person from being much more useful to the public. In such cases my resignation of life must not only be innocent but laudable. And most people who lie under any temptation to abandon existence, are in some such situation. Those, who have health, or power, or authority, have commonly better reason to be in humour with the world.

A man is engaged in a conspiracy for the public interest; is seized upon suspicion; is threatened with the rack; and knows from his own weakness that the secret will be extorted from him: Could such a one consult the public interest better than by putting a quick period to a miserable life? This was the case of the famous and brave *Strozi* of *Florence*.

Again, suppose a malefactor justly condemned to a shameful death; can any reason be imagined, why he may not anticipate his punishment, and save himself all the anguish of thinking on its dreadful approaches? He invades the business of providence no more than the magistrate did, who ordered his execution; and his voluntary death is equally advantageous to society by ridding it of a pernicious member.

That suicide may often be consistent with interest and with our duty to *ourselves*, no one can question, who allows that age, sickness, or misfortune may render life a burthen, and make it worse even than annihilation. I believe that no man ever threw away life, while it was worth keeping. For such is our natural horror of death, that small motives will never be able to reconcile us to it; and though perhaps the situation of a man's health or fortune did not seem to require this remedy, we may at least be assured, that any one who, without apparent reason, has had recourse to it, was curst with such an incurable depravity or gloominess of temper as must poison all enjoyment, and render him equally miserable as if he had been loaded with the most grievous misfortunes.

If suicide be supposed a crime, 'tis only cowardice can impel us to it. If it be no crime, both prudence and courage should engage us to rid ourselves at once of existence, when it becomes a burthen. 'Tis the only way that we can then be useful to society, by setting an example, which, if imitated, would preserve to every one his chance for happiness in life and would effectually free him from all danger or misery.[3]

3. It would be easy to prove that Suicide is as lawful under the *Christian* dispensation as it was to the heathens. There is not a single text of Scripture which prohibits it. That great and infallible rule of faith and practice which must controul all philosophy and human reasoning, has left us in this particular to our natural liberty. Resignation to providence is indeed recommended in Scripture; but that implies only submission to ills that are inavoidable, not to such as may be remedied by prudence or courage. *Thou shalt not kill* is evidently meant to exclude only the

killing of others over whose life we have no authority. That this precept, like most of the Scripture precepts, must be modified by reason and common sense, is plain from the practice of magistrates, who punish criminals capitally, notwithstanding the letter of the law. But were this commandment ever so express against Suicide, it would now have no authority, for all the law of *Moses* is abolished, except so far as it is established by the law of Nature. And we have already endeavoured to prove, that Suicide is not prohibited by that law. In all cases *Christians* and *Heathens* are precisely upon the same footing; *Cato* and *Brutus, Arria* and *Portia* acted heroically; those who now imitate their example ought to receive the same praises from posterity. The power of committing suicide is regarded by *Pliny* as an advantage which men possess even above the Deity himself. *God cannot even if he wishes to commit suicide, the supreme boon that he has bestowed among all of the penalties of life. Book II, chap. 5.*

AN ENQUIRY CONCERNING HUMAN UNDERSTANDING

Of Miracles[1]

PART I.

There is, in Dr. *Tillotson's* writings, an argument against the *real presence*, which is as concise, and elegant, and strong as any argument can possibly be supposed against a doctrine, so little worthy of a serious refutation. It is acknowledged on all hands, says that learned prelate, that the authority, either of the scripture or of tradition, is founded merely in the testimony of the apostles, who were eye-witnesses to those miracles of our Saviour, by which he proved his divine mission. Our evidence, then, for the truth of the *Christian* religion is less than the evidence for the truth of our senses; because, even in the first authors of our religion, it was no greater; and it is evident it must diminish in passing from them to their disciples; nor can anyone rest such confidence in their testimony, as in the immediate object of his senses. But a weaker evidence can never destroy a stronger; and therefore, were the doctrine of the real presence ever so clearly revealed in scripture, it were directly contrary to the rules of just reasoning to give our assent to it. It contradicts sense, though both the scripture and tradition, on which it is supposed to be built, carry not such evidence with them as sense; when they are considered merely as external evidences, and are not brought home to everyone's breast, by the immediate operation of the Holy Spirit.

Nothing is so convenient as a decisive argument of this kind, which must at least *silence* the most arrogant bigotry and superstition, and free us from their impertinent solicitations. I flatter myself, that I have discovered an argument of a like nature, which, if just,

1. [Dr. John Tillotson, 1630–1694, originally a Calvinist, became a moderate Anglican and rose to be Archbishop of Canterbury from 1691 to 1694. In his major work, *The Rule of Faith*, first published in 1666, and in his *Discourse against Transubstantiation*, 1684, he attacked the Roman Catholic doctrine that the body and blood of Jesus Christ are really present in the bread and wine at the conclusion of the Eucharistic service.]

will, with the wise and learned, be an everlasting check to all kinds of superstitious delusion, and consequently, will be useful as long as the world endures. For so long, I presume, will the accounts of miracles and prodigies be found in all history, sacred and profane.

Though experience be our only guide in reasoning concerning matters of fact; it must be acknowledged, that this guide is not altogether infallible, but in some cases is apt to lead us into errors. One, who in our climate, should expect better weather in any week of *June* than in one of *December*, would reason justly, and conformably to experience; but it is certain, that he may happen, in the event, to find himself mistaken. However, we may observe, that, in such a case, he would have no cause to complain of experience; because it commonly informs us beforehand of the uncertainty, by that contrariety of events, which we may learn from a diligent observation. All effects follow not with like certainty from their supposed causes. Some events are found, in all countries and all ages, to have been constantly conjoined together. Others are found to have been more variable, and sometimes to disappoint our expectations; so that, in our reasonings concerning matter of fact, there are all imaginable degrees of assurance, from the highest certainty to the lowest species of moral evidence.

A wise man, therefore, proportions his belief to the evidence. In such conclusions as are founded on an infallible experience, he expects the event with the last degree of assurance, and regards his past experience as a full *proof* of the future existence of that event. In other cases, he proceeds with more caution: He weighs the opposite experiments: He considers which side is supported by the greater number of experiments: To that side he inclines, with doubt and hesitation; and when at last he fixes his judgment, the evidence exceeds not what we properly call *probability*. All probability, then, supposes an opposition of experiments and observations, where the one side is found to overbalance the other, and to produce a degree of evidence, proportioned to the superiority. A hundred instances or experiments on one side, and fifty on another, afford a doubtful expectation of any event; though a hundred uniform experiments, with only one that is contradictory, reasonably beget a pretty strong degree of assurance. In all cases, we must balance the opposite experiments, where they are opposite, and deduct the smaller number from the greater, in order to know the exact force of the superior evidence.

To apply these principles to a particular instance; we may observe, that there is no species of reasoning more common, more

useful, and even necessary to human life, than that which is derived
from the testimony of men, and the reports of eye-witnesses and
spectators. This species of reasoning, perhaps, one may deny to be
founded on the relation of cause and effect. I shall not dispute about
a word. It will be sufficient to observe, that our assurance in any argument of this kind is derived from no other principle than our observation of the veracity of human testimony, and of the usual conformity of facts to the reports of witnesses. It being a general maxim,
that no objects have any discoverable connection together, and that
all the inferences, which we can draw from one to another, are
founded merely on our experience of their constant and regular
conjunction; it is evident, that we ought not to make an exception to
this maxim in favor of human testimony, whose connection with any
event seems, in itself, as little necessary as any other. Were not the
memory tenacious to a certain degree; had not men commonly an
inclination to truth and a principle of probity; were they not sensible to shame, when detected in a falsehood: Were not these, I say,
discovered by *experience* to be qualities, inherent in human nature,
we should never repose the least confidence in human testimony.
A man delirious, or noted for falsehood and villainy, has no manner of authority with us.

And as the evidence, derived from witnesses and human testimony, is founded on past experience, so it varies with the experience, and is regarded either as a *proof* or a *probability*, according as
the conjunction between any particular kind of report and any kind
of object has been found to be constant or variable. There are a
number of circumstances to be taken into consideration in all judgments of this kind; and the ultimate standard, by which we determine all disputes, that may arise concerning them, is always derived
from experience and observation. Where this experience is not entirely uniform on any side, it is attended with an unavoidable contrariety in our judgments, and with the same opposition and mutual destruction of argument as in every other kind of evidence. We
frequently hesitate concerning the reports of others. We balance the
opposite circumstances, which cause any doubt or uncertainty; and
when we discover a superiority on any side, we incline to it; but still
with a diminution of assurance, in proportion to the force of its antagonist.

This contrariety of evidence, in the present case, may be derived
from several different causes; from the opposition of contrary testimony; from the character or number of the witnesses; from the
manner of their delivering their testimony; or from the union of all

these circumstances. We entertain a suspicion concerning any matter of fact, when the witnesses contradict each other; when they are but few, or of a doubtful character; when they have an interest in what they affirm; when they deliver their testimony with hesitation, or on the contrary, with too violent asseverations. There are many other particulars of the same kind, which may diminish or destroy the force of any argument, derived from human testimony.

Suppose, for instance, that the fact, which the testimony. endeavors to establish, partakes of the extraordinary and the marvelous; in that case, the evidence, resulting from the testimony, admits of a diminution, greater or less, in proportion as the fact is more or less unusual. The reason, why we place any credit in witnesses and historians, is not derived from any *connection*, which we perceive *a priori*, between testimony and realty, but because we are accustomed to find a conformity between them. But when the fact attested is such a one as has seldom fallen under our observation, here is a contest of two opposite experiences; of which the one destroys the other, as far as its force goes, and the superior can only operate on the mind by the force, which remains. The very same principle of experience, which gives us a certain degree of assurance in the testimony of witnesses, gives us also, in this case, another degree of assurance against the fact, which they endeavor to establish; from which contradiction there necessarily arises a counterpoise, and mutual destruction of belief and authority.

I should not believe such a story were it told me by Cato; was a proverbial saying in Rome, even during the lifetime of that philosophical patriot.[2] The incredibility of a fact, it was allowed, might invalidate so great an authority.

The *Indian* prince, who refused to believe the first relations concerning the effects of frost, reasoned justly; and it naturally required very strong testimony to engage his assent to facts, that arose from a state of nature, with which he was unacquainted, and which bore so little analogy to those events, of which he had had constant and uniform experience. Though they were not contrary to his experience, they were not conformable to it.[3]

2. *Plutarch*, in vita Catonis Min. 19 [*Life of Cato* (the younger)].

3. No *Indian*, it is evident, could have experience that water did not freeze in cold climates. This is placing nature in a situation quite unknown to him; and it is impossible for him to tell *a priori* what will result from it. It is making a new experiment, the consequence of which is always uncertain. One may sometimes conjecture from analogy what will follow; but still this is but conjecture. And it must be confessed, that, in the present case of freezing, the event follows con-

But in order to increase the probability against the testimony of witnesses, let us suppose, that the fact, which they affirm, instead of being only marvelous, is really miraculous; and suppose also, that the testimony, considered apart and in itself, amounts to an entire proof; in that case, there is proof against proof, of which the strongest must prevail, but still with a diminution of its force, in proportion to that of its antagonist.

A miracle is a violation of the laws of nature; and as a firm and unalterable experience has established these laws, the proof against a miracle, from the very nature of the fact, is as entire as any argument from experience can possibly be imagined. Why is it more than probable, that all men must die; that lead cannot, of itself, remain suspended in the air; that fire consumes wood, and is extinguished by water; unless it be, that these events are found agreeable to the laws of nature, and there is required a violation of these laws, or in other words, a miracle to prevent them? Nothing is esteemed a miracle, if it ever happen in the common course of nature. It is no miracle that a man, seemingly in good health, should die on a sudden: because such a kind of death, though more unusual than any other, has yet been frequently observed to happen. But it is a miracle, that a dead man should come to life; because that has never been observed, in any age or country. There must, therefore, be a uniform experience against every miraculous event, otherwise the event would not merit that appellation. And as a uniform experience amounts to a proof, there is here a direct and full *proof*, from the nature of the fact, against the existence of any miracle; nor can such a proof be destroyed, or the miracle rendered credible, but by an opposite proof, which is superior.[4]

trary to the rules of analogy, and is such as a rational *Indian* would not look for. The operations of cold upon water are not gradual, according to the degrees of cold; but whenever it comes to the freezing point, the water passes in a moment, from the utmost liquidity to perfect hardness. Such an event, therefore, may be denominated *extraordinary*, and requires a pretty strong testimony, to render it credible to people in a warm climate: But still it is not *miraculous*, nor contrary to uniform experience of the course of nature in cases where all the circumstances are the same. The inhabitants of *Sumatra* have always seen water fluid in their own climate, and the freezing of their rivers ought to be deemed a prodigy: But they never saw water in *Muscovy* during the winter; and therefore they cannot reasonably be positive what would there be the consequence.

4. Sometimes an event may not, *in itself, seem* to be contrary to the laws of nature, and yet, if it were real, it might, by reason of some circumstances, be denominated a miracle; because, in *fact*, it is contrary to these laws. Thus if a person, claiming a divine authority, should command a sick person to be well, a healthful man to fall down dead, the clouds to pour rain, the winds to blow, in

The plain consequence is (and it is a general maxim worthy of our attention), 'That no testimony is sufficient to establish a miracle, unless the testimony be of such a kind, that its falsehood would be more miraculous, than the fact, which it endeavors to establish: And even in that case there is a mutual destruction of arguments, and the superior only gives us an assurance suitable to that degree of force, which remains, after deducting the inferior.' When anyone tells me, that he saw a dead man restored to life, I immediately consider with myself, whether it be more probable, that this person should either deceive or be deceived, or that the fact, which he relates, should really have happened. I weigh the one miracle against the other; and according to the superiority, which I discover, I pronounce my decision, and always reject the greater miracle. If the falsehood of his testimony would be more miraculous, than the event which he relates; then, and not till then, can he pretend to command my belief or opinion.

PART II.

In the foregoing reasoning we have supposed, that the testimony, upon which a miracle is founded, may possibly amount to an entire proof, and that the falsehood of that testimony would be a real prodigy: But it is easy to show, that we have been a great deal too liberal in our concession, and that there never was a miraculous event established on so full an evidence.

For *first*, there is not to be found, in all history, any miracle attested by a sufficient number of men, of such unquestioned good sense, education, and learning, as to secure us against all delusion in themselves; of such undoubted integrity, as to place them beyond all suspicion of any design to deceive others; of such credit and

short, should order many natural events, which immediately follow upon his command; these might justly be esteemed miracles, because they are really, in this case, contrary to the laws of nature. For if any suspicion remain, that the event and command concurred by accident, there is no miracle and no transgression of the laws of nature. If this suspicion be removed, there is evidently a miracle, and a transgression of these laws; because nothing can be more contrary to nature than that the voice or command of a man should have such an influence. A miracle may be accurately defined, *a transgression of a law of nature by a particular volition of the Deity, or by the interposition of some invisible agent.* A miracle may either be discoverable by men or not. This alters not its nature and essence. The raising of a house or ship into the air is a visible miracle. The raising of a feather, when the wind wants ever so little of a force requisite for that purpose, is as real a miracle, though not so sensible with regard to us.

reputation in the eyes of mankind, as to have a great deal to lose in case of their being detected in any falsehood; and at the same time, attesting facts, performed in such a public manner, and in so celebrated a part of the world, as to render the detection unavoidable: All which circumstances are requisite to give us a full assurance in the testimony of men.

Secondly. We may observe in human nature a principle, which, if strictly examined, will be found to diminish extremely the assurance, which we might, from human testimony, have, in any kind of prodigy. The maxim, by which we commonly conduct ourselves in our reasonings, is, that the objects, of which we have no experience, resemble those, of which we have; that what we have found to be most usual is always most probable; and that where there is an opposition of arguments, we ought to give the preference to such as are founded on the greatest number of past observations. But though, in proceeding by this rule, we readily reject any fact which is unusual and incredible in an ordinary degree; yet in advancing farther, the mind observes not always the same rule; but when anything is affirmed utterly absurd and miraculous, it rather the more readily admits of such a fact, upon account of that very circumstance, which ought to destroy all its authority. The passion of *surprise* and *wonder*, arising from miracles, being an agreeable emotion, gives a sensible tendency towards the belief of those events, from which it is derived. And this goes so far, that even those who cannot enjoy this pleasure immediately, nor can believe those miraculous events, of which they are informed, yet love to partake of the satisfaction at second-hand or by rebound, and place a pride and delight in exciting the admiration of others.

With what greediness are the miraculous accounts of travelers received, their descriptions of sea and land monsters, their relations of wonderful adventures, strange men, and uncouth manners? But if the spirit of religion join itself to the love of wonder, there is an end of common sense; and human testimony, in these circumstances, loses all pretensions to authority. A religionist may be an enthusiast, and imagine he sees what has no reality: He may know his narrative to be false, and yet persevere in it, with the best intentions in the world, for the sake of promoting so holy a cause: Or even where this delusion has not place, vanity, excited by so strong a temptation, operates on him more powerfully than on the rest of mankind in any other circumstances; and self-interest with equal force. His auditors may not have, and commonly have not, sufficient judgment to canvass his evidence: What judgment they

have, they renounce by principle, in these sublime and mysterious
subjects: Or if they were ever so willing to employ it, passion and a
heated imagination disturb the regularity of its operations. Their
credulity increases his impudence: And his impudence overpow-
ers their credulity.

Eloquence, when at its highest pitch, leaves little room for reason or reflection; but addressing itself entirely to the fancy or the
affections, captivates the willing hearers, and subdues their understanding. Happily, this pitch it seldom attains. But what a *Tully* or a
Demosthenes could scarcely effect over a *Roman* or *Athenian* audi-
ence, every *Capuchin*, every itinerant or stationary teacher can perform over the generality of mankind, and in a higher degree, by
touching such gross and vulgar passions.

The many instances of forged miracles, and prophecies, and supernatural events, which, in all ages, have either been detected by
contrary evidence, or which detect themselves by their absurdity,
prove sufficiently the strong propensity of mankind to the extraordinary and the marvelous, and ought reasonably to beget a suspicion against all relations of this kind. This is our natural way of
thinking, even with regard to the most common and most credible
events. For instance: There is no kind of report, which rises so easily, and spreads so quickly, especially in country places and provin-
cial towns, as those concerning marriages; insomuch that two young
persons of equal condition never see each other twice, but the
whole neighborhood immediately join them together. The pleasure
of telling a piece of news so interesting, of propagating it, and of
being the first reporters of it, spreads the intelligence. And this is so
well known, that no man of sense gives attention to these reports,
till he find them confirmed by some greater evidence. Do not the
same passions, and others still stronger, incline the generality of
mankind to believe and report, with the greatest vehemence and
assurance, all religious miracles?

Thirdly. It forms a strong presumption against all supernatural
and miraculous relations, that they are observed chiefly to abound
among ignorant and barbarous nations; or if a civilized people has
ever given admission to any of them, that people will be found to
have received them from ignorant and barbarous ancestors, who
transmitted them with that inviolable sanction and authority,
which always attend received opinions. When we peruse the first
histories of all nations, we are apt to imagine ourselves transported
into some new world; where the whole frame of nature is dis-
jointed, and every element performs its operations in a different

manner, from what it does at present. Battles, revolutions, pestilence, famine, and death, are never the effect of those natural causes, which we experience. Prodigies, omens, oracles, judgments, quite obscure the few natural events, that are intermingled with them. But as the former grow thinner every page, in proportion as we advance nearer the enlightened ages, we soon learn, that there is nothing mysterious or supernatural in the case, but that all proceeds from the usual propensity of mankind towards the marvelous, and that, though this inclination may at intervals receive a check from sense and learning, it can never be thoroughly extirpated from human nature.

It is strange, a judicious reader is apt to say, upon the perusal of these wonderful historians, *that such prodigious events never happen in our days.* But it is nothing strange, I hope, that men should lie in all ages. You must surely have seen instances enough of that frailty. You have yourself heard many such marvelous relations started, which, being treated with scorn by all the wise and judicious, have at last been abandoned even by the vulgar. Be assured, that those renowned lies, which have spread and flourished to such a monstrous height, arose from like beginnings; but being sown in a more proper soil, shot up at last into prodigies almost equal to those which they relate.

It was a wise policy in that false prophet, *Alexander,* who, though now forgotten, was once so famous, to lay the first scene of his impostures in *Paphlagonia,* where, as *Lucian* tells us, the people were extremely ignorant and stupid, and ready to swallow even the grossest delusion. People at a distance, who are weak enough to think the matter at all worth enquiry, have no opportunity of receiving better information. The stories come magnified to them by a hundred circumstances. Fools are industrious in propagating the imposture; while the wise and learned are contented, in general, to deride its absurdity, without informing themselves of the particular facts, by which it may be distinctly refuted. And thus the impostor above-mentioned was enabled to proceed, from his ignorant *Paphlagonians,* to the enlisting of votaries, even among the *Grecian* philosophers, and men of the most eminent rank and distinction in *Rome*: Nay, could engage the attention of that sage emperor *Marcus Aurelius*; so far as to make him trust the success of a military expedition to his delusive prophecies.

The advantages are so great, of starting an imposture among an ignorant people, that, even though the delusion should be too gross to impose on the generality of them (*which, though seldom, is some-*

times the case) it has a much better chance for succeeding in remote countries, than if the first scene had been laid in a city renowned for arts and knowledge. The most ignorant and barbarous of these barbarians carry the report abroad. None of their countrymen have a large correspondence, or sufficient credit and authority to contradict and beat down the delusion. Men's inclination to the marvelous has full opportunity to display itself. And thus a story, which is universally exploded in the place where it was first started, shall pass for certain at a thousand miles distance. But had *Alexander* fixed his residence at *Athens*, the philosophers of that renowned mart of learning had immediately spread, throughout the whole *Roman* empire, their sense of the matter; which, being supported by so great authority, and displayed by all the force of reason and eloquence, had entirely opened the eyes of mankind. It is true, *Lucian*, passing by chance through *Paphlagonia*, had an opportunity of performing this good office. But, though much to be wished, it does not always happen, that every *Alexander* meets with a *Lucian*, ready to expose and detect his impostures.

I may add as a *fourth* reason, which diminishes the authority of prodigies, that there is no testimony for any, even those which have not been expressly detected, that is not opposed by an infinite number of witnesses; so that not only the miracle destroys the credit of testimony, but the testimony destroys itself. To make this the better understood, let us consider, that, in matters of religion, whatever is different is contrary; and that it is impossible the religions of ancient *Rome*, of *Turkey*, of *Siam*, and of *China* should, all of them, be established on any solid foundation. Every miracle, therefore, pretended to have been wrought in any of these religions (and all of them abound in miracles), as its direct scope is to establish the particular system to which it is attributed; so has it the same force, though more indirectly, to overthrow every other system. In destroying a rival system, it likewise destroys the credit of those miracles, on which that system was established; so that all the prodigies of different religions are to be regarded as contrary facts, and the evidences of these prodigies, whether weak or strong, as opposite to each other. According to this method of reasoning, when we believe any miracle of *Mahomet* or his successors, we have for our warrant the testimony of a few barbarous *Arabians*: And on the other hand, we are to regard the authority of *Titus Livius*, *Plutarch*, *Tacitus*, and, in short, of all the authors and witnesses, *Grecian*, *Chinese*, and *Roman Catholic*, who have related any miracle in their particular religion; I say, we are to regard their testimony in the same light as if they had mentioned that *Mahometan* miracle, and had in express terms contradicted it, with the same certainty as they have for the miracle they relate. This argument may appear oversubtle and refined; but is not in reality different from the reasoning of a judge, who supposes, that the credit of two witnesses, maintaining a crime against anyone, is destroyed by the testimony of two others, who affirm him to have been two hundred leagues distant, at the same instant when the crime is said to have been committed.

One of the best attested miracles in all profane history, is that which *Tacitus* reports of *Vespasian*, who cured a blind man in *Alexandria*, by means of his spittle, and a lame man by the mere touch of his foot; in obedience to a vision of the god *Serapis*, who had enjoined them to have recourse to the Emperor, for these miraculous cures. The story may be seen in that fine historian,[5] where every circumstance seems to add weight to the testimony, and might be displayed at large with all the force of argument and eloquence, if anyone were now concerned to enforce the evidence of that exploded and idolatrous superstition. The gravity, solidity, age, and probity of so great an emperor, who, through the whole course of his life, conversed in a familiar manner with his friends and courtiers, and never affected those extraordinary airs of divinity assumed by *Alexander* and *Demetrius*. The historian, a cotemporary writer, noted for candor and veracity, and withal, the greatest and most penetrating genius, perhaps, of all antiquity; and so free from any tendency to credulity, that he even lies under the contrary imputation, of atheism and profaneness: The persons, from whose authority he related the miracle, of established character for judgment and veracity, as we may well presume; eye-witnesses of the fact, and confirming their testimony, after the *Flavian* family was despoiled of the empire, and could no longer give any reward, as the price of a lie. *Utrumque, qui interfuere, nunc quoque memorant, postquam nullum mendacio pretium.*[6] To which if we add the public nature of the facts, as related, it will appear, that no evidence can well be supposed stronger for so gross and so palpable a falsehood.

There is also a memorable story related by Cardinal *de Retz*, which may well deserve our consideration. When that intriguing

5. Hist. Bk. IV, chap. 81. Suetonius gives nearly the same account *in vita Vesp.* [*Lives of the Twelve Caesars*, Bk. VIII].

6. [Of each event, those who were present, even now keep speaking, though they get no reward for lying.]

politician fled into *Spain*, to avoid the persecution of his enemies, he passed through *Saragossa*, the capital of Aragon, where he was shown, in the cathedral, a man, who had served seven years as a door-keeper, and was well known to everybody in town, that had ever paid his devotions at that church. He had been seen, for so long a time, wanting a leg; but recovered that limb by the rubbing of holy oil upon the stump; and the cardinal assures us that he saw him with two legs. This miracle was vouched by all the canons of the church; and the whole company in town were appealed to for a confirmation of the fact; whom the cardinal found, by their zealous devotion, to be thorough believers of the miracle. Here the relater was also cotemporary to the supposed prodigy, of an incredulous and libertine character, as well as of great genius; the miracle of so *singular* a nature as could scarcely admit of a counterfeit, and the witnesses very numerous, and all of them, in a manner, spectators of the fact, to which they gave their testimony. And what adds mightily to the force of the evidence, and may double our surprise on this occasion, is, that the cardinal himself, who relates the story, seems not to give any credit to it, and consequently cannot be suspected of any concurrence in the holy fraud. He considered justly, that it was not requisite, in order to reject a fact of this nature, to be able accurately to disprove the testimony, and to trace its falsehood, through all the circumstances of knavery and credulity which produced it. He knew, that, as this was commonly altogether impossible at any small distance of time and place; so was it extremely difficult, even where one was immediately present, by reason of the bigotry, ignorance, cunning, and roguery of a great part of mankind. He therefore concluded, like a just reasoner, that such an evidence carried falsehood upon the very face of it, and that a miracle, supported by any human testimony, was more properly a subject of derision than of argument.

There surely never was a greater number of miracles ascribed to one person, than those, which were lately said to have been wrought in *France* upon the tomb of Abbé *Paris*, the famous *Jansenist*, with whose sanctity the people were so long deluded. The curing of the sick, giving hearing to the deaf, and sight to the blind, were everywhere talked of as the usual effects of that holy sepulchre. But what is more extraordinary; many of the miracles were immediately proved upon the spot, before judges of unquestioned integrity, attested by witnesses of credit and distinction, in a learned age, and on the most eminent theater that is now in the world. Nor is this all: A relation of them was published and dispersed everywhere; nor

were the *Jesuits*, though a learned body, supported by the civil magistrate, and determined enemies to those opinions, in whose favor
the miracles were said to have been wrought, ever able distinctly to
refute or detect them.[7] Where shall we find such a number of circumstances, agreeing to the corroboration of one fact? And what
have we to oppose to such a cloud of witnesses, but the absolute im-

7. This book was writ by Mons. *Montgeron*, counselor or judge of the parliament of *Paris*, a man of figure and character, who was also a martyr to the cause,
and is now said to be somewhere in a dungeon on account of his book.

There is another book in three volumes (called *Recueil des Miracles de l'Abbé
Paris*) giving an account of many of these miracles, and accompanied with prefa-
tory discourses, which are very well written. There runs, however, through the
whole of these a ridiculous comparison between the miracles of our Savior and
those of the Abbé; wherein it is asserted, that the evidence for the latter is equal
to that for the former: As if the testimony of men could ever be put in the balance with that of God himself, who conducted the pen of the inspired writers. If
these writers, indeed, were to be considered merely as human testimony, the
French author is very moderate in his comparison: since he might, with some
appearance of reason, pretend, that the *Jansenist* miracles much surpass the
other in evidence and authority. The following circumstances are drawn from
authentic papers, inserted in the above-mentioned book.

Many of the miracles of Abbé *Paris* were proved immediately by witnesses
before the officiality or bishop's court at *Paris*, under the eye of cardinal *Noailles*,
whose character for integrity and capacity was never contested even by his enemies.

His successor in the archbishopric was an enemy to the *Jansenists*, and for
that reason promoted to the see by the court. Yet 22 rectors or *curés* of *Paris*, with
infinite earnestness, press him to examine those miracles, which they assert to
be known to the whole world, and undisputably certain: But he wisely forbore.

The *Molinist* party had tried to discredit these miracles in one instance, that
of Madamoiselle *le Franc*. But, besides that their proceedings were in many respects the most irregular in the world, particularly in citing only a few of the
Jansenist witnesses, whom they tampered with: Besides this, I say, they soon
found themselves overwhelmed by a cloud of new witnesses, one hundred and
twenty in number, most of them persons of credit and substance in *Paris*, who
gave oath for the miracle. This was accompanied with a solemn and earnest
appeal to the parliament. But the parliament were forbidden by authority to
meddle in the affair. It was at last observed, that where men are heated by zeal
and enthusiasm, there is no degree of human testimony so strong as may not
be procured for the greatest absurdity: And those who will be so silly as to examine the affair by that medium, and seek particular flaws in the testimony, are
almost sure to be confounded. It must be a miserable imposture, indeed, that
does not prevail in that contest.

All who have been in *France* about that time have heard of the reputation of
Mons. *Heraut*, the *lieutenant de Police*, whose vigilance, penetration, activity, and
extensive intelligence have been much talked of. This magistrate, who by the
nature of his office is almost absolute, was invested with full powers, on purpose to suppress or discredit these miracles; and he frequently seized immedi-

possibility or miraculous nature of the events, which they relate?
And this surely, in the eyes of all reasonable people, will alone be
regarded as a sufficient refutation.

Is the consequence just, because some human testimony has the
utmost force and authority in some cases, when it relates the battle
of *Philippi* or *Pharsalia* for instance; that therefore all kinds of testimony must, in all cases, have equal force and authority? Suppose
that the *Caesarean* and *Pompeian* factions had, each of them, claimed
the victory in these battles, and that the historians of each party had
uniformly ascribed the advantage to their own side; how could
mankind, at this distance, have been able to determine between
them? The contrariety is equally strong between the miracles related by *Herodotus* or *Plutarch*, and those delivered by *Mariana, Bede,*
or any monkish historian.

The wise lend a very academic faith to every report which favors
the passion of the reporter; whether it magnifies his country, his
family, or himself, or in any other way strikes in with his natural inclinations and propensities. But what greater temptation than to
appear a missionary, a prophet, an ambassador from heaven? Who
would not encounter many dangers and difficulties, in order to at-

---

ately, and examined the witnesses and subjects of them: But never could reach
anything satisfactory against them.

In the case of Madamoiselle *Thibaut* he sent the famous *De Sylva* to examine
her; whose evidence is very curious. The physician declares, that it was impossible she could have been so ill as was proved by witnesses; because it was impossible she could, in so short a time, have recovered so perfectly as he found
her. He reasoned, like a man of sense, from natural causes; but the opposite
party told him, that the whole was a miracle, and that his evidence was the very
best proof of it.

The *Molinists* were in a sad dilemma. They durst not assert the absolute insufficiency of human evidence, to prove a miracle. They were obliged to say, that
these miracles were wrought by witchcraft and the devil. But they were told, that
this was the resource of the *Jews* of old.

No *Jansenist* was ever embarrassed to account for the cessation of the
miracles, when the churchyard was shut up by the king's edict. It was the touch
of the tomb, which produced these extraordinary effects; and when no one
could approach the tomb, no effects could be expected. God, indeed, could have
thrown down the walls in a moment; but he is master of his own graces and
works, and it belongs not to us to account for them. He did not throw down the
walls of every city like those of *Jericho*, on the sounding of the rams' horns, nor
break up the prison of every apostle, like that of St. *Paul.*

No less a man, than the Duc de *Chatillon*, a duke and peer of *France*, of the
highest rank and family, gives evidence of a miraculous cure, performed upon
a servant of his, who had lived several years in his house with a visible and palpable infirmity.

tain so sublime a character? Or if, by the help of vanity and a heated imagination, a man has first made a convert of himself, and entered seriously into the delusion; who ever scruples to make use of pious frauds, in support of so holy and meritorious a cause?

The smallest spark may here kindle into the greatest flame; because the materials are always prepared for it. The *avidum genus auricularum*, the gazing populace, receive greedily, without examination, whatever soothes superstition, and promotes wonder.

How many stories of this nature, have, in all ages, been detected and exploded in their infancy? How many more have been celebrated for a time, and have afterwards sunk into neglect and oblivion? Where such reports, therefore, fly about, the solution of the phenomenon is obvious; and we judge in conformity to regular experience and observation, when we account for it by the known and natural principles of credulity and delusion. And shall we, rather than have a recourse to so natural a solution, allow of a miraculous violation of the most established laws of nature?

I need not mention the difficulty of detecting a falsehood in any private or even public history, at the place, where it is said to hap-

---

I shall conclude with observing, that no clergy are more celebrated for strictness of life and manners than the secular clergy of *France*, particularly the rectors or curés of *Paris*, who bear testimony to these impostures.

The learning, genius, and probity of the gentlemen and the austerity of the nuns of *Port-Royal*, have been much celebrated all over *Europe*. Yet they all give evidence for a miracle, wrought on the niece of the famous *Pascal*, whose sanctity of life, as well as extraordinary capacity, is well known. The famous *Racine* gives an account of this miracle in his famous history of *Port-Royal*, and fortifies it with all the proofs, which a multitude of nuns, priests, physicians, and men of the world, all of them of undoubted credit, could bestow upon it. Several men of letters, particularly the bishop of *Tournay*, thought this miracle so certain, as to employ it in the refutation of atheists and free-thinkers. The queen-regent of *France*, who was extremely prejudiced against the *Port-Royal*, sent her own physician to examine the miracle, who returned an absolute convert. In short, the supernatural cure was so uncontestable, that it saved, for a time, that famous monastery from the ruin with which it was threatened by the *Jesuits*. Had it been a cheat, it had certainly been detected by such sagacious and powerful antagonists, and must have hastened the ruin of the contrivers. Our divines, who can build up a formidable castle from such despicable materials; what a prodigious fabric could they have reared from these and many other circumstances, which I have not mentioned! How often would the great names of *Pascal*, *Racine*, *Arnaud*, *Nicole*, have resounded in our ears? But if they be wise, they had better adopt the miracle, as being more worth, a thousand times, than all the rest of their collection. Besides, it may serve very much to their purpose. For that miracle was really performed by the touch of an authentic holy prickle of the holy thorn, which composed the holy crown, which, &c.

pen; much more when the scene is removed to ever so small a distance. Even a court of judicature, with all the authority, accuracy,
and judgment, which they can employ, find themselves often at a
loss to distinguish between truth and falsehood in the most recent
actions. But the matter never comes to any issue, if trusted to the
common method of altercation and debate and flying rumors; especially when men's passions have taken part on either side.

In the infancy of new religions, the wise and learned commonly
esteem the matter too inconsiderable to deserve their attention or
regard. And when afterwards they would willingly detect the cheat,
in order to undeceive the deluded multitude, the season is now past,
and the records and witnesses, which might clear up the matter,
have perished beyond recovery.

No means of detection remain, but those which must be drawn
from the very testimony itself of the reporters: And these, though
always sufficient with the judicious and knowing, are commonly too
fine to fall under the comprehension of the vulgar.

Upon the whole, then, it appears, that no testimony for any kind
of miracle has ever amounted to a probability, much less to a proof;
and that, even supposing it amounted to a proof, it would be opposed by another proof; derived from the very nature of the fact,
which it would endeavor to establish. It is experience only, which
gives authority to human testimony; and it is the same experience,
which assures us of the laws of nature. When, therefore, these two
kinds of experience are contrary, we have nothing to do but subtract
the one from the other, and embrace an opinion, either on one side
or the other, with that assurance which arises from the remainder.
But according to the principle here explained, this subtraction, with
regard to all popular religions, amounts to an entire annihilation;
and therefore we may establish it as a maxim, that no human testimony can have such force as to prove a miracle, and make it a just
foundation for any such system of religion.

I beg the limitations here made may be remarked, when I say,
that a miracle can never be proved, so as to be the foundation of a
system of religion. For I own, that otherwise, there may possibly be
miracles, or violations of the usual course of nature, of such a kind
as to admit of proof from human testimony; though, perhaps, it will
be impossible to find any such in all the records of history. Thus,
suppose, all authors, in all languages, agree, that, from the first of
January 1600, there was a total darkness over the whole earth for
eight days: Suppose that the tradition of this extraordinary event is
still strong and lively among the people: That all travelers, who re-

turn from foreign countries, bring us accounts of the same tradition, without the least variation or contradiction: It is evident, that our present philosophers, instead of doubting the fact, ought to receive it as certain, and ought to search for the causes whence it might be derived. The decay, corruption, and dissolution of nature, is an event rendered probable by so many analogies, that any phenomenon, which seems to have a tendency towards that catastrophe, comes within the reach of human testimony, if that testimony be very extensive and uniform.

But suppose, that all the historians who treat of *England*, should agree, that, on the first of *January* 1600, Queen *Elizabeth* died; that both before and after her death she was seen by her physicians and the whole court, as is usual with persons of her rank; that her successor was acknowledged and proclaimed by the parliament; and that, after being interred a month, she again appeared, resumed the throne, and governed *England* for three years: I must confess that I should be surprised at the concurrence of so many odd circumstances, but should not have the least inclination to believe so miraculous an event. I should not doubt of her pretended death, and of those other public circumstances that followed it: I should only assert it to have been pretended, and that it neither was, nor possibly could be real. You would in vain object to me the difficulty, and almost impossibility of deceiving the world in an affair of such consequence; the wisdom and solid judgment of that renowned queen; with the little or no advantage which she could reap from so poor an artifice: All this might astonish me; but I would still reply, that the knavery and folly of men are such common phenomena, that I should rather believe the most extraordinary events to arise from their concurrence, than admit of so signal a violation of the laws of nature.

But should this miracle be ascribed to any new system of religion; men, in all ages, have been so much imposed on by ridiculous stories of that kind, that this very circumstance would be a full proof of a cheat, and sufficient, with all men of sense, not only to make them reject the fact, but even reject it without farther examination. Though the Being to whom the miracle is ascribed, be, in this case, Almighty, it does not, upon that account, become a whit more probable; since it is impossible for us to know the attributes or actions of such a Being, otherwise than from the experience which we have of his productions, in the usual course of nature. This still reduces us to past observation, and obliges us to compare the instances of the violation of truth in the testimony of men, with those of the violation of the laws of nature by miracles, in order to judge which of them is most likely and probable. As the violations of truth are more common in the testimony concerning religious miracles, than in that concerning any other matter of fact, this must diminish very much the authority of the former testimony, and make us form a general resolution, never to lend any attention to it, with whatever specious pretense it may be covered.

Lord *Bacon* seems to have embraced the same principles of reasoning. 'We ought,' says he, 'to make a collection or particular history of all monsters and prodigious births or productions, and in a word of everything new, rare, and extraordinary in nature. But this must be done with the most severe scrutiny, lest we depart from truth. Above all, every relation must be considered as suspicious, which depends in any degree upon religion, as the prodigies of *Livy*: And no less so, everything that is to be found in the writers of natural magic or alchemy, or such authors, who seem, all of them, to have an unconquerable appetite for falsehood and fable.[8]

I am the better pleased with the method of reasoning here delivered, as I think it may serve to confound those dangerous friends or disguised enemies to the *Christian Religion*, who have undertaken to defend it by the principles of human reason. Our most holy religion is founded on *Faith*, not on reason; and it is a sure method of exposing it to put it to such a trial as it is, by no means, fitted to endure. To make this more evident, let us examine those miracles, related in scripture; and not to lose ourselves in too wide a field, let us confine ourselves to such as we find in the *Pentateuch*, which we shall examine, according to the principles of these pretended Christians, not as the word or testimony of God himself, but as the production of a mere human writer and historian. Here then we are first to consider a book, presented to us by a barbarous and ignorant people, written in an age when they were still more barbarous, and in all probability long after the facts which it relates, corroborated by no concurring testimony, and resembling those fabulous accounts, which every nation gives of its origin. Upon reading this book, we find it full of prodigies and miracles. It gives an account of a state of the world and of human nature entirely different from the present: Of our fall from that state: Of the age of man, extended to near a thousand years: Of the destruction of the world by a deluge: Of the arbitrary choice of one people, as the favorites of heaven; and that people the countrymen of the author: Of their deliverance from

8. Nov. Org. lib, ii. aph. 29.

bondage by prodigies the most astonishing imaginable: I desire anyone to lay his hand upon his heart, and after a serious consideration declare, whether he thinks that the falsehood of such a book, supported by such a testimony, would be more extraordinary and miraculous than all the miracles it relates; which is, however, necessary to make it be received, according to the measures of probability above established.

What we have said of miracles may be applied, without any variation, to prophecies; and indeed, all prophecies are real miracles, and as such only, can be admitted as proofs of any revelation. If it did not exceed the capacity of human nature to foretell future events, it would be absurd to employ any prophecy as an argument for a divine mission or authority from heaven. So that, upon the whole, we may conclude, that the *Christian Religion* not only was at first attended with miracles, but even at this day cannot be believed by any reasonable person without one. Mere reason is insufficient to convince us of its veracity: And whoever is moved by *Faith* to assent to it, is conscious of a continued miracle in his own person, which subverts all the principles of his understanding, and gives him a determination to believe what is most contrary to custom and experience.